£3.50

THE ROYAL
WORLD OF ANIMALS

THE ROYAL
WORLD
OF ANIMALS

BEATRICE CAYZER

SIDGWICK & JACKSON
LONDON

First published in Great Britain in 1989 by
Sidgwick & Jackson Limited
1 Tavistock Chambers, Bloomsbury Way
London WC1A 2SG

ISBN 0 283 99857 1

Photoset by Rowland Phototypesetting Limited
Bury St Edmunds, Suffolk
Printed and bound in Great Britain by
Butler and Tanner Limited, Frome and London

CONTENTS

INTRODUCTION

Animals have always been associated with royalty and the aristocracy. As far back as 1066 the Norman knights brought their hunting hawks with them in the invasion fleet, and the speed and manoeuvrability of William the Conqueror's horsemen contributed to the defeat of the Saxon infantry. For sport, for war, for travelling from place to place, for protection and for companionship animals were indispensable to the new King of England and his nobles.

This book covers only the Royal House of Windsor, from Queen Victoria to the present day. There are many other royal connections with animals down the centuries, but they would require a book of their own if full justice were to be done to them. The early Norman kings kept lions – then a far more exotic creature than the familiar safari park sight of today. Much later George IV kept a menagerie in his private retreat at Virginia Water in Surrey. And Alexandra, the beautiful, sad, deaf queen of the pleasure-loving Edward VII, assuaged her loneliness with a mini-zoo at Sandringham, containing tropical birds, an Egyptian ram, a tame bear and a cage of monkeys.

The royal love affair with horse-racing probably began with Good Queen Bess, who attended the races at Stratford. Her successor, James I, was so enthusiastic that he established the sport at Newmarket, the town near Cambridgeshire that is still synonymous with horse-breeding and racing nearly four centuries later. His grandson, Charles II, who gave his name to a breed of spaniels, raced there – as have the Prince of Wales and the Princess Royal in our own times. Edward VII was the royal horse-owner par excellence – in terms of victories. He won the Derby on three occasions, a race that to this day has eluded his great-granddaughter the Queen, an equally enthusiastic and knowledgeable follower of the Turf.

We have come a long way since the invading Norman knights led their chargers off the boats on to the Sussex beaches. Today's royalty no longer dons plumed helmets to joust on richly caparisoned steeds – but Princess Anne in hard hat and jodhpurs at Burghley, or her brother charging up the polo field at Smith's Lawn, are just as fearless and determined as their medieval counterparts. Swift deerhounds no longer outpace the game in the royal forests – but faithful, well-trained labradors still retrieve royal pheasants shot on Scottish game moors. Royalty no longer turns out, hawk on gauntleted wrist, to see sharp-eyed birds swoop down on unsuspecting pigeons – indeed, the Queen is likely to be saddened if some wild bird of prey cuts short the career of one of her Sandringham-bred prize racing pigeons.

The Queen's conservation-minded husband and eldest son, for their part, are likely to feel some sympathy for the hawk – for with modern

The Prince and Princess of Wales with Prince William and Prince Harry are greeted by a ram at the Royal Tournament, 1988.

farming techniques many birds of prey have become endangered species. Prince Philip's and the Prince of Wales's work for ecological causes, for the balance between man's requirements and those of the environment, have helped to bring these issues into the public eye and given them much-needed publicity. In the late twentieth century the relationship between royalty and animals continues, but the emphasis is constantly shifting to reflect the changing circumstances of the planet which we all, royalty and commoners, share.

1
VICTORIA AND ALBERT
'No horse, no review!'

Princess Victoria was only eighteen when she ascended the throne of England in 1837, on the death of her childless uncle, William IV. Born and brought up at Kensington Palace, then the rather dilapidated home of various lesser members of the royal family, she had had a lonely, unhappy childhood. Her father, the impoverished Duke of Kent, had died when Victoria was an infant. 'Ma was never very fond of me,' she said of the German-born Duchess who had fallen under the sinister influence of her ambitious Comptroller, Sir John Conroy. Victoria's affections were centred on her governess, Baroness Lehzen, and Dash, the little King Charles spaniel which, apart from her mother's parakeet and a tame canary, was her only playmate.

The future Queen kept a journal in which she recorded affairs of state that were to have a bearing on her destiny, as well as the small succession of events that made up her restricted daily life. 'I dressed dear, sweet little Dash in a scarlet jacket and blue trousers,' she wrote when she was thirteen, and for Christmas she noted that she gave him three india rubber balls and two pieces of gingerbread decorated with candles and holly. Dash later repaid his mistress's affection by jumping into the sea and swimming after her yacht. When she was ill he 'spent his little life' in her room.

As soon as Victoria became Queen and moved from Kensington Palace, one of her major concerns was to settle Dash in at Buckingham Palace. She was pleased to find that he was soon 'quite happy in the garden'. The little spaniel led a privileged existence. He was included in the daily conferences that the new Queen held with her Prime Minister, Lord Melbourne, and rose to the occasion by licking Melbourne's hand. Another admirer was Lord Conyngham, the Lord Chamberlain, who fondled Dash and sent his children to play with him in the Long Gallery at Windsor Castle. The Conyngham children, who called Victoria 'The Tween', enjoyed glorious romps in the 500-foot-long Gallery with Dash and his royal mistress.

On the morning of her coronation, 28 June 1838, Victoria was awoken at four o'clock by a salute of guns in the park. It was to be a long day. At the end of the five-hour ceremony in Westminster Abbey she was driven home in state to Buckingham Palace. Once inside, she immediately gathered up her skirts and ran to her room to give Dash a bath before the evening's festivities began.

A lonely figure at the age of 14, Princess Victoria's main companion was the King Charles spaniel she described in her diary as 'Dear Sweet Little Dash'. On the day of her Coronation, Victoria gave him a bath.

Riding was one of the young Queen's chief pleasures, and the best rides were duly recorded in her journal. A typical entry read: 'It was a delightful ride. We cantered a good deal. Sweet little Rosy went beautifully.' The daily routine scarcely varied. The mornings were devoted to affairs of state with Lord Melbourne, whom Victoria came to regard as a father figure, and in the afternoons the whole court went out riding, with the Queen heading the cavalcade. At Windsor, Melbourne brought his own horses. With the amiable Prime Minister beside her, these rides became the Queen's favourite recreation; often they galloped for miles without pulling up.

The Queen was small and inclined to be plump, and her tiny stature looked well on horseback. At her best in a black velvet riding habit with top hat and a veil over her fair hair, she attracted much attention. An early admirer was Lord Alfred Paget, a Gentleman of the Household who often accompanied her on the afternoon rides and owned a retriever called Mrs Bumps. Both dog and owner wore the Queen's portrait in lockets.

The high spot of her first year as Queen came when she reviewed her troops on horseback at Windsor, wearing an adapted military uniform with the Order of the Garter. In the early days of her reign none of Queen Victoria's public appearances was rehearsed, and it was pot luck whether she could manage to control her charger, Leopold, for two-and-a-half hours standing still. On this occasion, she not only managed to do so but afterwards went straight out for a canter on a favourite mare called Barbara. Known to be unpredictable, Barbara often played up. But the young Victoria was endowed with great surplus energy: she often danced until the early hours of the morning, and enjoyed mastering a difficult horse. Another incentive was to demonstrate her expertise to Lord Melbourne. Earlier in the year, the Prime Minister had thought that she would be unable to hold her horse when reviewing her troops in Hyde Park. His suggestion that she went in a carriage instead was met with the firm response: 'No horse, there will be no review!'

Backed up by the Duchess of Kent, who thought that her daughter should never appear in public without a lady-in-waiting by her side – which would not have been possible had the Queen been on horseback – Melbourne cancelled the review. News of the argument reached the press, and the battle royal at the Palace became the subject of a verse which started: 'I will have a horse, I'm determined on that.' Even if she did not win her first battle, Victoria's subjects were heartened to know that she was capable of standing up to her Prime Minister and to the unpopular Duchess of Kent.

By the end of 1838, Victoria was counting 'The Very Great Blessings' she had received during her wonderful coronation year. Far from giving any hint of the recluse she was later to become, the young Queen seemed to revel in her state duties. Freedom from the domination of her mother, and of Conroy, was one great blessing. Another was the opportunity to acquire as many animals as she chose.

Dash still reigned supreme in the Queen's heart; but, once her fondness for dogs became known, she was given many others. Among them was Laddie, a Scotch terrier. 'You'll be smothered with dogs,' warned Lord Melbourne. Victoria could not think of a happier fate.

*

*The young Queen Victoria riding out with her Prime Minister,
Melbourne, and her pet dogs.*

By the time she was nineteen, Victoria's advisers decided that another
great blessing should be added to her life: marriage. 'A woman,' said
Lord Melbourne, 'cannot stand alone for long, whatever situation she
is in.' Enjoying her new life to the full, Victoria was inclined to
disagree. It had long been suggested that when she became Queen she
should wed her cousin Prince Albert, from the German duchy of
Saxe-Coburg-Gotha. Victoria was to make the final choice; and, as his
visit approached, she grew less and less enthusiastic. As it turned out,
10 October 1839 was a date the young Queen was never to forget.

Arriving at Windsor Castle on the appointed day, poor Albert was
pale from sea-sickness after a turbulent crossing. All the same, his
manly good looks made an immediate impression on Victoria. 'It was
with some emotion that I beheld Albert – who is *beautiful*,' she wrote
in her journal. Falling immediately under the spell of this handsome
young prince, three months younger than herself but with an
advanced intelligence of which she stood in awe, Victoria was proud to
ride with him at her side in the afternoon cavalcade. Later, there was a
splendid ball. As no man was yet deemed fit to encircle the Queen's
waist with his arm, they had to sit out the waltzes; but Albert had no
need of the letter of recommendation he had brought with him from
King Leopold of Belgium, Victoria's favourite uncle. She was in love.

In short, Victoria found everything about Albert fascinating to the last degree. Not least was his gentle, silver-streaked black greyhound Eos (meaning 'dawn'), which had come with him from Coburg and which walked round the luncheon table offering her paw and eating from a fork.

The match, which already had Uncle Leopold's approval, required an official proposal from Victoria. Four days after his arrival, Victoria sent Albert a message asking him to visit her in a room known as the Blue Closet. 'I said to him that I thought he must be aware of why I had sent for him and told him that it would make me *too happy* if he would consent to what I wished,' she wrote later. There was no need for further words. Cutting short the awkwardness of the proposal, Albert took her in his arms and told her in German of his longing to spend his life with her. He had expected a wilful and imperious queen; instead, he had found an unspoilt girl longing for affection. And in Albert, Victoria had found the love of her life.

They had many tastes in common, and after their wedding in 1840 one of their happiest pastimes was to sketch together. Victoria was a talented artist. Her drawings of favourite animals were etched by Albert, and many of the results are remarkably professional. Among the pets immortalized in drawings and paintings was Eos, which came with them on honeymoon at Windsor. Dachshunds were among the many breeds which Queen Victoria cherished, and a drawing of one of her favourites, etched for her by the Prince in their wedding year, is still in the royal collections.

The year ended with two major events, one joyful, the other sad. The birth of the first of Victoria and Albert's nine children, Vicky, the Princess Royal, was followed a few weeks later by the death of the Queen's beloved childhood companion. Victoria never forgot Dash. He was buried at Windsor under a marble effigy bearing the inscription:

Here lies DASH
The favourite spaniel of Her Majesty Queen Victoria
In his 10th year.

Although Dash was never to be entirely replaced in her affections, Victoria took pleasure in acquiring dogs of a variety of breeds. Dachshunds, Skye terriers, scotties, Pomeranians, Pekineses, pugs, King Charles spaniels, Maltese terriers and collies – Queen Victoria went in for them all at one time or another. Albert, on the other hand, liked greyhounds and beagles. All their dogs were recorded on paper and canvas, in marble and bronze, by famous artists of the day such as Sir Edwin Landseer and Richard Westall. A favourite terrier, painted by Landseer, was called Islay. Melbourne, who was a great tease, said he had a low opinion of this dog – but allowed him to jump on his lap and lick his spectacles!

*Victoria as a widow, on horseback at Osborne. Attending her are
her daughter Princess Louise and the favoured John Brown.*

Of all Queen Victoria's dogs, Looty had the most dramatic history.
He had been one of the treasured Chinese imperial breed of Pekinese,
which lived in the Summer Palace at Peking. In the Taiping Rebellion
of 1864 he had been found by looters after the suicide of the aunt of the
Emperor of China, and rescued by British soldiers. Rather than set
eyes on 'the foreign devils', Looty's owner had killed herself, leaving
her five frenziedly barking dogs to guard her body. The brave survi-

vors were brought to Britain where Looty, a fawn and white specimen, was presented to the Queen. This was the start of a British craze for Pekinese dogs – Victoria soon found that, whichever breed she chose, it subsequently became very popular. Collies, for instance, were working sheepdogs when Victoria first saw them in the Highlands of Scotland; but after she acquired one as a household pet, a collie named Southport Perfection changed hands for the then dizzy sum of £1000.

Much later, after Albert's death, during a visit to Florence in 1883 Victoria saw a Pomeranian and decided to breed them for herself. In those days Poms were very much bigger than they are now – Victoria's first acquisition weighed nearly 30 lb, and bore a strong resemblance to a ragged-looking sheep. But in every litter Pomeranians tended to produce one or two pups which were miniatures, and it was these from which Victoria bred. At the first Crufts dog show, in 1891, the Queen showed six Poms – Fluffy, Nino, Mino, Beppo, Gilda and Lulu – all of which won prizes. For a while her only rival in the field was a Miss Hamilton of Bath, who specialized in white Pomeranians; Queen Victoria went in for a rainbow of colours from golden, orange and sable to blue, so as not to compete with Miss Hamilton. Charles Cruft also persuaded the Queen to exhibit Darnley, one of her collies. Another special pet was a fawn pug named Bully, but he was too unruly to be shown.

Queen Victoria's success as a dog breeder led the way for other members of her family to compete at dog shows. Following in her footsteps was her daughter-in-law Queen Alexandra, who showed basset hounds; while her grandson George V showed labradors. The tradition was carried on by her great-grandsons, including the Duke of Windsor, but has lapsed with the present generation of royalty.

Throughout Albert's lifetime, the Queen was ever sensitive to his humiliating constitutional position. One of the worst moments had been when the King of Prussia gave precedence to a mere Austrian archduke over the husband of the Queen of England. She gave Albert the title of Prince Consort, but he continued to be regarded by the British as a foreign upstart, whose only claim to distinction was that he had happened to marry the Queen of England. Albert, for all his noble qualities, was never deferred to as Victoria would have wished. But in 1843 his performance with the Belvoir Hunt did wonders for his popularity. The Queen was amazed. Albert was not generally interested in hunting, and the last thing she wanted him to do was to take it up as a hobby. 'One can scarcely credit the absurdity of people here,' she wrote to her uncle, King Leopold. 'Albert's riding so boldly and hard has made such a sensation that it has been written about all over the country and they make much more of it than if he had done some great act.'

*Queen Victoria's love of animals was passed on to her family. One of
her favourite pictures was of her grand-daughter, Princess Alice
Mary Victoria with pet terrier.*

Albert, in fact, was by no means insignificant and made many
important contributions to the scientific and artistic development of
the country. The Great Exhibition of 1851 was his brain-child, and at
Osborne, on the Isle of Wight, he transformed a nondescript house into
an Italianate villa of continuing architectural interest. Apart from his
agricultural improvements at Windsor, his biggest enterprise was the
creation of a more distant sanctuary in the Scottish Highlands:

Balmoral. In a small house near Braemar Albert saw the potential for a royal residence set in acres of natural beauty which reminded him of his native Germany. Several generations of British royalty now have reason to be grateful for his foresight. Albert pulled down the original house and replaced it with a castle of his own design. Built of granite in Scottish baronial style, it was habitable by 1855; and, with the development of the railways (another of Albert's interests), it offered an accessible retreat for the ever-growing family, their dogs, horses and entourage.

Here, Victoria could dote on Albert and enjoy family life without distractions. Running out of doors in all weathers to sketch and walk, with her children and dogs, Victoria (like her successors) could enjoy a life of family privacy. She rode Highland ponies, drove a trap and confessed that every year 'my heart becomes more fixed in this dear paradise'.

The paradise was to outlast its creator. Overwork and anxiety had robbed the Prince of his youthful good looks, and as he approached forty he began to suffer from a variety of ailments. Early in 1861 he died of typhoid fever. Victoria was inconsolable. In mourning for ten years, she became known as the widow of Windsor due to her reclusive habits, although in fact she spent as much time as possible in the two country retreats hallowed by Albert's memory; Osborne and Balmoral.

In old age, her children grown up and married, the Queen turned once more to the consolation of animals. All the companions of the past had been drawn, painted or sculpted, so that the favourite dogs and horses of her youth would never be forgotten. Her abiding love of animals made her particularly interested in the kennels and stables at each of her royal residences and, although in virtual retirement, she kept a very firm hand on all that concerned them. She was rarely un-accompanied by several dogs at a time, and was also very fond of her ponies and horses, always referring to them by name. Among her favourites at Balmoral were several sturdy Highland ponies – a sure-footed breed that will take a rider to the most precipitous places without the slightest trouble.

Nevertheless, in 1868 Queen Victoria had the idea that her ponies were being overworked. She instructed Frederick Ponsonby, then a junior equerry, to allow only those guests who 'understood horses' to ride them. This put the unfortunate Ponsonby in an awkward position. According to the Queen, none of the guests then staying at the Castle was fit to take out a pony without close supervision, which was not always possible. The first to be refused a pony from the royal stables was Edgar Boehm, an eminent sculptor who had instructed the Queen's daughter Princess Louise. Among other guests to come under the royal ban were Canon Duckworth, a friend of the Prince of Wales,

Queen Victoria at Balmoral, clutching Turi the white Pomeranian who was with her when she died at Osborne four years later. In attendance are the Duchess of Roxburghe, Mistress of the Robes, Victoria's Highland attendant George Gordon and Indian servant Mohammed Ismail. The carriage, now preserved at Windsor, is drawn by Victoria's favourite white pony, Bella.

and Hermann Sahl, the German secretary employed to draft the Queen's letters to foreign sovereigns.

All three were deeply offended, and poor Ponsonby was unable to give a proper explanation, as the Queen had sworn him to confidentiality. Boehm threatened to go home if he was not allowed to ride, and the others sent letters of protest, complaining about Ponsonby's insolence. The Queen was undoubtedly much amused by their complaints, but she had saved her dear hill ponies from any possible harm or overwork; to her, that was far more important than the wounded feelings of her guests.

The widow of Osborne lived to a ripe old age, celebrating her Diamond Jubilee in 1897 and seeing in the twentieth century. In 1901, as she lay dying in the Italianate villa that her beloved Albert had created on the Isle of Wight, she rallied enough to ask her doctor if she was any better. Assured cautiously that she was, Victoria made her last request: 'Then may I have little Turi?'

The family hurried to bring her the miniature Pomeranian which had been a devoted companion. But, unlike Dash who had spent hours at her bedside during a childhood illness, Turi lay unwillingly on her bed. Shortly after he had made his escape, the old Queen drew her last breath.

2

EDWARD VII AND ALEXANDRA

'I am Caesar, the King's dog.'

To many of the subjects of her far-flung empire, Queen Victoria's eldest son and heir was known as the Prince of Pleasure. Fifty before Victoria allowed him to see state papers, and almost sixty by the time he became King, Edward VII passed most of his life in what his mother described as 'a whirl of amusements'.

Married at the age of twenty-one to the beautiful eighteen-year-old Princess Alexandra of Denmark, Edward – always known to his family as Bertie – became one of the best shots in the country, bred one famous Derby winner and owned three in all. Edwardian England delighted in his fashionable appearance, his charm and geniality, and the legendary hospitality to be found at Sandringham House, the estate in Norfolk where he and Alexandra entertained the nobility and kept a menagerie of animals.

Edwardian society grew well used to turning a blind eye to Bertie's extra-marital adventures – as did his frequently lonely wife. The truth was that Bertie was easily bored. Craving constant variety, he had a string of stylish mistresses with whom he let himself be seen quite openly until the end of his life. His last holiday was spent at the fashionable French resort of Biarritz with the astute and fascinating Mrs Keppel – 'Beloved Alice'.

On their walks together they were always accompanied by the King's long-haired fox terrier, Caesar, on which Edward doted. His collar bore the inscription: 'I am Caesar, the King's dog.' Not a particularly well-behaved animal, Caesar would gnaw chair legs and shoes and frequently disobeyed the King's commands. But whatever he did, Caesar's loyalty and affection for his master outweighed all faults so far as Edward was concerned. As the King's chauffeur, Stamper, wrote later: 'His Majesty never beat Caesar. The dog and he were devoted to one another. It was a picture to see him shaking his stick at the dog when he had done wrong. "You naughty dog," he would say very slowly. "You naughty, naughty dog." And Caesar would then wag his tail.'

At Biarritz, the King's days were given over to recreation. The French understood his need for privacy, and together with Caesar he and Mrs Keppel would visit select restaurants where he could indulge his appreciation of gourmet food untroubled by the curious. On one occasion, when they were lunching at the fashionable Café Glatzen,

King Edward VII in Biarritz with his favourite dog, Caesar.
Written on Caesar's collar were the words 'I am the King's dog'.
Shortly before this picture was taken, Caesar had escaped to romp
in the sea.

Caesar's behaviour threatened to draw unwelcome attention to his royal owner. 'Caesar, Caesar. Come here!' shouted the King suddenly, startling the guests as he rose to his feet. The terrier was busily chasing a white peacock and resolutely refused to obey his master. Stamper was called to run in pursuit, and, having eventually captured the recalcitrant dog, was told to lock him in the car as a punishment. Caesar's outraged barks and whines continued to be heard throughout the meal. Jaunty, mischievous, cheerful and totally loyal, Caesar gave Edward what his courtiers were not always ready to offer: unconditional admiration combined with a capricious streak which amused the King.

At night, the dog slept curled up in an armchair beside the King's bed. 'Do you like your old master?' he would ask him sentimentally, waiting for a last wag of the tail before putting out the light. In the morning Wellard, the second footman, would come and take Caesar out for a quick walk, then wash and comb him. At breakfast Caesar, as immaculate as his owner, would be sitting by the table awaiting his first titbit of the day. Seen in all the best places, Caesar went everywhere with the King. Pictured on the royal yacht *Britannia*, he stands proudly next to his master and the future Edward VIII – 'little David'.

Bertie always felt he had been denied maternal affection. When he was a child, Victoria described him as 'slow and stupid'. Put under the stern supervision of Baron Stockmar, Victoria's political adviser, he had a series of tutors. But he was an unwilling pupil. From the first Prince Albert had imposed idealistic standards for the upbringing of the heir to the throne which his son failed to meet. Bertie was only too well aware that his parents regarded him as a failure; and neither parent understood his longing for affection. Victoria made various attempts to show her son in an idealistic light. She sketched him in his nursery with a huge white pet rabbit, and later commissioned Winterhalter to paint him dressed in a Highland kilt with a dog. In both cases the animals looked more like props than the flesh-and-blood pets that Bertie longed for as companions.

At Balmoral, Bertie was introduced to riding by a new tutor, Frederick Gibbs. There was an unlucky beginning when his first pony ran away with him, but Gibbs persevered. Gibbs thought that the Prince had been confined with his books too much. 'The Prince of Wales has not been in a good state,' he wrote. 'I advised that he should be taken deer-stalking as much as possible.'

And so Bertie started on the lifelong pursuit of game. He began by carrying a large stick on his shoulder and was taught to slither through the undergrowth to track deer. Soon he was given proper guns and trained to shoot deer with a rifle. He walked his retrievers to bag

Queen Alexandra with grandchildren and an assortment of dogs at Sandringham. Top left, a collie escapes from the royal kennels which are still used today for the Queen's labradors.

grouse and pheasants with a 12-bore shotgun.

By the age of seventeen, Bertie had also become an excellent horseman. At first, he had been prevented from hunting in England largely because his mother feared he would meet a frivolous set in the hunting field. But, evading parental control, he joined the South Oxfordshire Hunt. How he loved soaring over fences like Pegasus, the mythical winged horse. Here he met the nucleus of the circle his mother most deplored: those fast-riding and equally fast-living members of the aristocracy who were later known as the Marlborough House set – named after Bertie's London residence.

In vain did Victoria pray that Bertie 'might become like his dear Papa' – high-minded and hard-working. He was sent to both Oxford and Cambridge for short and unproductive periods. Then came various tours of foreign countries. At the age of nineteen, he was allowed to spend ten weeks with the Grenadier Guards in Ireland. This comparative freedom, which Victoria and Albert later bitterly regretted, led to a brief affair with an aspiring actress called Nellie Clifden. The shock of the scandal caused Victoria to blame Bertie for his father's failing health and subsequent early death.

The seventeen-year-old Princess Alexandra of Denmark had been selected by Prince Albert shortly before his death as the future wife who would make Bertie settle down. 'I looked to his wife as being *His Salvation*,' wrote Victoria, referring to Alexandra as 'a pearl *not to be lost*'. Conveniently overlooked was the fact that, although Bertie became almost immediately susceptible to the charms of the sports-minded young princess, the attractions of an early marriage did not hold quite such a strong appeal.

The second of six children, Alexandra had been brought up in an unsophisticated way by her parents, Prince and Princess Christian of Denmark. The Prince had neither the estates nor the income to correspond with his royal title. But if money was in short supply, Alexandra, known to her family as Alix, enjoyed an idyllic childhood. Long, happy summers were spent at one of the King's estates outside Copenhagen, where she learned to ride as fast as the north wind. Here Alix and her brothers and sisters wandered with their dogs and her favourite pet donkey.

An early impression of the young Princess Alix was given by Miss Bessie Carew, who was visiting Copenhagen in 1854:

> My attention was caught by the sight of a rather unusual equipage. We saw a go-cart drawn by a goat which was led by a very smart-looking footman in green and gold livery, with another one behind. Seated in the cart was the most beautiful little girl, about eight years old, wearing a little fur bonnet. She waved to us gaily as she went by.

This was the first recorded comment on the two characteristics which everyone later noted: her exquisite beauty and her lively spontaneous courtesy.

Bertie had first met Alexandra apparently by chance at Speyer Cathedral in Germany; in fact it had been engineered by Victoria. He met her again in Belgium, where she was staying with her family. The seventeen-year-old Princess owned no jewels and wore only a plain dress; the effect was one of breathtaking simplicity and loveliness, and Bertie, struck by her simple dignity, proposed at once. The wedding took place at St George's Chapel, Windsor, in 1863, with the bride a picture of innocence and grace in white Honiton lace.

It was not just her beauty but also her unstudied charm of manner that had already endeared Alexandra to the British public. During the procession into London on the day of her arrival from Denmark, she had performed an instinctive action which immediately won all hearts. The streets had been packed with such crowds that several times the procession came to a halt. At one point, a charger ridden by an officer in the Household Cavalry began to buck and kick, catching its hoof in the spokes of a rear wheel of the carriage. It seemed inevitable that the excited animal would break its leg, but Princess

Queen Alexandra, (third from right, seated) with her sister, the Czarina, Czar Alexander III, their children and members of the court. Anastasia, the Czar's grand-daughter, took her spaniel Jimmy with her to Ekaterinburg where he perished in the revolution with the Russian Imperial Family.

Alexandra calmly leaned out from the carriage and, taking hold of the animal's hoof, eased it from the wheel. Bertie was overcome. Here was a wife he could admire wholeheartedly.

One of Bertie's first projects as a husband was an ambitious programme of rebuilding and renovation at Sandringham, the Norfolk estate purchased shortly before he had proposed to Alexandra. He started with new stabling for some thirty horses and coach-houses for fifteen carriages. At the house itself the reception rooms were to be enlarged, while the Prince considered a new wing to be added to the south. Developing what was rather poor agricultural farmland into one of the greatest shoots in England, Bertie continued to buy in more farms and cottages; for the next ten years or more he was regularly in debt to the tune of £20,000 a year – a lot of money in those days.

While news reached Queen Victoria's ears of the late hours and gambling enjoyed by the Prince of Wales and his house guests, Alexandra for her part shocked her mother-in-law by hunting when expecting a baby. It was the excitement of 'a screaming scent when the hounds fairly flew' that Alexandra enjoyed – while hoping at the same time that 'the poor fox' would escape. Victoria tried her best to forbid Alexandra's hunting, writing that everyone was shocked by risks to which the Princess of Wales was exposing herself in following the hounds. In fact, Alexandra soon had to give up. Then as now, a member of the royal family out hunting proved a magnet to sightseers. Hundreds of horsemen and carriages blocked the lanes; on one occasion one of them bumped into the Prince of Wales's horse and unseated him. When she could not hunt, the Princess would drive herself to a meet unannounced. A striking figure in immaculate black costume and tilted top hat, she was an expert whip, given to driving her ponies with dash and verve.

But Queen Victoria was soon to have a deeper cause for dissatisfaction. While 'poor, dear Alix never once complained', it was becoming obvious that the Prince was involved with other women. His affair with the actress Lillie Langtry was one of the first of a series of blatant infidelities which the Prince did little to conceal.

By 1866 Alexandra had given birth to three children, the third of whom, Prince Eddy, was destined to die of pneumonia at the age of twenty-eight. Some time after his birth, when the Princess allegedly contracted rheumatic fever in the damp Sandringham climate, it became obvious that she was going deaf. It had a serious effect on her life and relationships. Today, this type of deafness – inherited from her mother – responds to treatment; but then all Alexandra could do was disguise the handicap. Few people outside their immediate circle ever knew of her problem. But the rheumatic fever, which left her permanently lame in one leg, caused her to make alterations to her side-saddle. Continuing to go as fast as her horses would carry her, Alexandra now rode on the off-side. This was duly noted by members of the hunt, and of the court.

As Victoria was not slow to admit, Bertie was hardly the ideal husband. But, refusing to allow jealousy to corrode what to her was a basically happy home, Alexandra took a genuine joy in her surroundings as well as in their inhabitants, human and animal. In return, her husband treated her with consideration and courtesy, making very sure that other people did the same.

On his return from a nine-month visit to India in 1875, he brought with him a cargo of lavish gifts, curiosities and animals. Sandringham, which Alexandra had already turned into a private menagerie, was never the same again. Among the animals were some Himalayan bears, for whom a special bear pit was dug. Unfortunately Charlie and Polly grew unreliable, and eventually had to be sent to London Zoo. The children were given a miniature Indian pony called Nawab, which was so small and neat-footed that he could be ridden in the house. Alexandra took particular pleasure in the character and training of Nawab: 'The dear little Indian pony came all the way upstairs into my dressing-room, and walked down again, like a Christian,' she wrote to her closest son, the future George V.

Earlier, in the winter of 1868–9 during her long-awaited trip to

Left, *Often pictured cuddling cats and dogs, Alexandra devoted her affections to a wide variety of animals during her husband's frequent absences. Her menagerie included a pet monkey and a cage of parakeets.*
Right, *A portrait of the Princess of Wales in 1894 by Sir Luke Fildes. Alexandra's pet spaniel Joss chased the train and disappeared when she left London on a visit to her sister in Russia.*

Egypt with the Prince of Wales, Alexandra had acquired a huge black ram. She had rescued it from being butchered, because it had proved itself so tame as to eat out of her hand. Alexandra first insisted that the ram accompany them on one of the boats in their convoy up the Nile. The sailors garlanded its neck with flowers in her honour. Finally she begged to have it brought back to England, where it took up residence at Sandringham.

Birds had a special fascination for the family, and the children awoke in the morning to the crowing of prize bantams. A friend sent forty white cockatoos, which were accommodated in an artistically designed aviary. A lake, complete with island, was made in the park for a picturesque crane. A gift of Belgian-bred racing pigeons started another royal sporting tradition. They won several races for Edward and Alexandra, flying on one occasion from the Shetlands to Sandringham in ten hours. Their descendants are now kept in a pigeon loft near Kings Lynn, and are visited by the Queen and Prince Philip when at Sandringham. They support themselves by the production of saleable eggs and hatched birds, as well as winning numerous trophies.

. THREE PONIES ON THE BALMORAL ROAD . AVGVST. 1870 .
" LA FIERTE."   " LA STUPIDITE."   " LA GOURMANDISE "

A drawing by Arthur Ellis of the Princess of Wales, her lady in waiting Miss Charlotte Knollys, and himself, riding along the Balmoral road.

The menagerie continued to escalate, for during his long absences from Sandringham Bertie often despatched animals home with full instructions for their upkeep. 'We went to see some Brahmin cows which dear Papa sent from India,' wrote the eleven-year-old Prince George to his grandmother. A special cage was built for a family of monkeys (though, like the bears, they ended up at the zoo). A new pony stable was erected, with each door bearing the name of its occupant painted in gold.

Everywhere there were animals to be seen. A green parrot in the hall who repeated 'Am I not beautiful?' was trained to shout 'Three cheers for the Queen' when Victoria was persuaded to make one of her rare visits. She disapproved of Bertie's extravagance at Sandringham, where he was constantly expanding and embellishing the estate, and feared that Eddy and George would be corrupted by the 'fast set' who visited at weekends. The old Queen wrote in no uncertain terms to say that young boys should be kept apart from the society of the fashionable people who comprised the Prince of Wales's set.

Increasingly isolated by her deafness from the smart repartee and sprightly conversation of the friends who so enlivened Bertie's days, Alexandra turned more and more to the simple pleasures brought by children and animals. Her favourite horse was a mare called Viva, and for her Silver Wedding her children gave her a silver statuette of the animal, which took pride of place on her dressing table. Her dressing room was a clutter of bric-à-brac, family photographs and Fabergé objects which had become dear to her. Perched in the middle was an elderly and ferocious white cockatoo which pecked at visitors but took sugar from his mistress.

Alexandra's love of animals was instinctive. Unlike our present Queen she had little knowledge of scientific breeding principles, but took a delight in cherishing whatever came her way. Any stray dog found wandering on the estate was taken in and cared for in the kennels. For Alexandra and her children, their visit to the kennels was the high spot of the day. Dog biscuits had yet to be invented and they would feed the animals with cubes of bread.

At one time the keeper had in his charge as many as sixty dogs of various breeds. There were the borzois and Russian wolfhounds which were gifts from the Tsar. Other occupants included great danes, bulldogs, Clumber spaniels, dachshunds, Scotch deerhounds, black pugs and terriers, Chinese chows, Pomeranians and Pekes as well as several mongrels. At one time there was also a samoyed from an Arctic expedition, and a thirteen-stone St Bernard; not to mention Luska, a Siberian sledge dog, who worried Alexandra by refusing to eat until it was discovered that she had been brought up on a diet of rice and fish.

The kennels at Sandringham are still in use. Of a size equalled only by those of a professional breeder, they are now used for the Sandringham gun dogs. The Queen's children and shooting party guests leave their labradors, hounds and terriers there when visiting.

Alexandra's personal pets and house dogs included tiny Japanese spaniels and the rather larger basset hounds. The bassets had a distinguished pedigree. As Queen, Alexandra showed them at the 53rd Dog Exhibition at the Crystal Palace in 1908, where they won her no fewer than four first prizes.

Her lasting favourite was a spaniel called Joss. When she went from Victoria Station on the first lap of her journey to Russia to visit her widowed sister, the Dowager Empress Marie Feodorovna, she let her eldest daughter, Princess Louise, bring Joss along to see her leave. As her train drew away, Alexandra leaned out of the carriage to wave goodbye. Taking this as a signal to follow, Joss slipped his collar and scampered off in pursuit of the train, gathering speed as his mistress disappeared from sight. Princess Louise eventually recovered the dog and, knowing that her mother would be frantic with anxiety, she gathered courage to ask Queen Victoria to send a telegram so that news of Joss's safe recovery would be relayed to 'Motherdear', as her five children called Alix.

In her old age, Alexandra had to battle with her advisers to continue to keep her dogs in the manner to which they had grown accustomed.

Alexandra as Queen in 1904 with two of her spaniels aboard the royal yacht.

'My kennels and my stables I will not have touched,' she exclaimed when urged to economize. She was begged to 'put down' worn-out horses and aged dogs, but refused. Even the scarcity of manpower during World War I did not alter her determination. She said: 'It breaks my heart that this cruel beastly war should be the cause of so many of my precious old friends and horses being slaughtered after all these years of faithful service.' Some of the horses went. But no amount of persuasion could change her resolve regarding the aged dogs. When a dog did die it was always distressing. Little headstones at Marlborough House and Sandringham bear testimony to the sad passing of Blackie, Zero and Tiny Muff, among the much loved family pets.

Alexandra's enjoyment of country life was entirely different from Bertie's. She went round the estate in a carriage drawn by her Hungarian ponies, sometimes driving herself and other times being driven by a Hungarian coachman. She loved sights such as the herd of web-antlered Japanese deer emerging from the mists. Bertie's country pursuits, on the other hand, were more organized.

Like everything he did, Edward's shooting was ordered on a grand scale. His shoots were arranged on the lines of the 'battue' system, with scores of beaters driving the birds towards the guns. A pheasant shoot, for which the birds had often been hand-reared in coops, would yield a thousand head or more. A bag of partridges was also numbered in hundreds after a day's shooting.

Few people were more generous hosts than the Prince of Wales. Shooting luncheons were taken in a specially erected marquee. In the evenings, long and convivial dinners was followed by cards played late into the night. The provision of first-class shooting facilities at Sandringham was probably part of Edward's notion of unlimited hospitality, although the shooting of birds was much criticized at the time, especially by the tenant farmers who complained that it interfered with their crops.

The breeding of racehorses, such as those on the stud farm built at nearby Wolferton, increasingly engaged the Prince's interest.

In 1890 alone, he attended twenty-eight race meetings at courses around Britain. The year before his accession to the throne, he headed the list of winning owners. That year, 1900, his winnings totalled £29,586 – almost as much as his Civil List allowance.

Persimmon was the Prince of Wales's greatest horse. As a two-year-old he won first at Ascot, then at Goodwood. The following season saw a royal triumph when Persimmon won the 1896 Derby for his delighted owner. Bertie told friends that Persimmon's wins had paid for the laying out of new gardens at Sandringham. Further wins, which included the Eclipse Stakes and the St Leger, brought in enough money to finance the impressive range of glasshouses at

Albert Edward, Prince of Wales, with the first of his three Derby winners, Persimmon, in 1897. With them are trainer, R. Marsh and jockey T. Watts. Later Persimmon became a renowned stallion, siring many winners and outliving his proud owner.

Sandringham, known as the Persimmon greenhouses. Edward planted a banana grove in them which produced clusters of fruit for admiring visitors, to whom bananas were then an exotic novelty. Persimmon continued to prove his worth when he was sent to stud, heading the list of leading sires in 1902, 1906, 1908 and 1912. He sired ninety-seven winners in all, whose prize money totalled £232,477.

In 1900 Bertie had his second Derby win, with Diamond Jubilee. Half-brother to Persimmon, Diamond Jubilee was out of the same mare, Perdita II. Diamond Jubilee's success gave Bertie a record of two Derbys out of the same mare; and the Triple Crown, thanks to his winning the Two Thousand Guineas and St Leger. It was a spectacular year for his racing luck – he also won the 1900 Grand National with Ambush II.

At Bertie's training stables at Egerton House near Newmarket hopes rose that the King, as he now was, would bring off the hat-trick by winning the 1909 Derby with Minoru, a horse which had already shown great promise. All hopes were justified, and great was the excitement when his royal owner led Minoru into the winner's enclosure. Heartening cries of 'Good Old Teddy', 'God Save the King' and 'We'll bail you out' erupted from the throats of thousands of loyal racegoers. It was probably the moment of peak popularity in his reign.

The cry about bailing him out was uncomfortably close to the truth.

Although Edward's personal finances had improved markedly since his accession to the throne, Egerton House had fallen on bad times. Help emerged from a surprising quarter – his former mistress, Lillie Langtry, who had herself become a racehorse owner. Bertie still cared deeply for Lillie and always listened to what she had to say. She explained that if he didn't continue to keep his horses at Egerton House, he would lose the special mile-and-a-quarter gallops of moss litter which had helped turn Minoru into a winner. With the aid of Leopold de Rothschild, one of the King's financial advisers, Egerton House was rescued and the royal horses continued to benefit from those mossy gallops.

One day, late in his career as a sire, Persimmon broke his pelvis. The King had the horse hung in slings to try and save him, but it was to no avail. Deeply distressed, the King had no option but to agree that the gallant Persimmon should be put down. Bertie commissioned an immense bronze statue of him as a memorial, which still dominates the stud farm at Sandringham.

Despite his wayward habits and self-indulgent manner of life, the key to Bertie's character was softness of heart. He would do almost

The Prince and Princess of Wales shortly after their marriage, riding in Hyde Park with the Duke of Cambridge and 'Affie', Edward's younger brother, the Duke of Edinburgh. Speculation that Affie was in love with the Princess, caused Victoria to marry him off to Marie of Russia.

*Alexandra, an accomplished horsewoman, was scolded by Victoria
for hunting when pregnant. After suffering a serious bout of
rheumatic fever, Alexandra changed to riding on the 'offside' of her
side-saddle due to a permanently stiff knee.*

anything for a friend in trouble; and where his animals were
concerned no expense was spared on their welfare. On a visit to
Marienbad in 1907, his dog Caesar became ill. The King's private
secretary, Frederick Ponsonby, was instructed to send to London for
the Royal vet, Sewell. When it was discovered that Sewell was about to
make a charge of £200 for coming out, Ponsonby argued with the King
on the grounds of extravagance. But His Majesty said that if his dog

was ill he would get the very best man and did not care what it cost. Luckily a first-class vet was found in Vienna who came and treated Caesar, who was back to normal within a couple of days.

The King's brief reign ended on his death in 1910. After the three-day lying-in-state at Westminster Hall, the huge and formal funeral procession took place with Edward's favourite charger, Kildare, being led behind the coffin. Following him was Bertie's adored fox terrier Caesar, led by a kilted Highlander. Then, and only then, followed the crowned heads of Europe. The faithful Caesar became an immediate celebrity. It was an age of sentiment, and a popular book about him was published, entitled *Where's Master?*

For poor Caesar, this was indeed a poignant question. Wandering disconsolately around the widowed Queen's belongings, which after nine years were being moved from Buckingham Palace back to Marlborough House, he seemed unable to settle. Perhaps because he had shared too many of his master's illicit intimate moments, Caesar appeared to be the one animal on which Alexandra could not lavish her affection.

A clue to Caesar's fate was hinted at when Margot Asquith called on Alix during the early days of her widowhood. She said of Caesar: 'Poor little dog. His devotion to your King, Ma 'am, touched every spectator.'

The Princess of Wales at Abergeldie in Scotland with Prince Eddy (who died in 1892) and Prince George (later George V), taken in 1866. Placed in panniers, the two little princes were taken by pony to join a picnic on the moor.

3
GEORGE V AND QUEEN MARY

'Thirty pounds is as much as I ever paid for a polo pony.'

A countryman at heart, George V was a man of simple tastes. There was a pleasant undercurrent of domesticity at York Cottage on the Sandringham estate where, for over thirty years of his marriage to the stately Princess May of Teck, King George felt more at home than in any palace.

'Our dear old home, I am sad at leaving it,' he wrote when he eventually left the cramped quarters of the estate cottage for the big house. There the widowed Queen Alexandra had lived on until 1925 with her tiny entourage, welcoming the six grandchildren whom she called the 'Georgie pets'. To the last, she still kept a menagerie of animals, and thought of her son – the King – as a small boy.

As it was for his father before him, Sandringham would always be George's favourite home. But George preferred the unpretentious and

Charlotte, George V's parrot, was allowed the freedom of the breakfast table.

King George with his famous shooting pony, Jock. When the King died, shortly after this picture was taken, Jock followed his coffin on the first stage of the funeral journey to the railway station at Sandringham.

well-ordered existence of a country squire. He was not above rabbiting with the keepers, fishing alone, or merely rambling through the marshes. One of the fifteen thousand wedding presents he had received on his marriage to May had been a cow. Because George had been brought up to know the elements of farming and stock breeding, he then set about buying the best stock to establish his future herds. His bull, Royal Crimson, was twice reserve champion. He paid top price for heifers of the Red Poll breed at a show in Ipswich.

George inherited his father's stables along with the 20,000-acre estate, and his racing fortunes peaked in 1928 when his bay filly Scuttle won the One Thousand Guineas. This was to be his only classic win. He ended his reign having bred the winners of some 135 races, earning £91,478 in prize money.

Unlike Edward VII, his son was not keen to spend large sums of money on buying horses. When told that the New York millionaire Stephen Sanford's father had bought a polo pony for £1200, King George remarked: 'Dear me, thirty pounds is as much as I ever paid for a polo pony.' An abstemious punter, he bet £1 on a 25-to-1 winner at the 1924 Grand National. Yet he settled a racing debt for £1000 which his brother-in-law, Prince Francis of Teck, had incurred at the Curragh.

George's schoolboyish sense of humour was in evidence when his horse Glastonbury was beaten in a close finish by Lord Rosebery's Midlothian, and he subsequently telegraphed to Rosebery: 'Confound Midlothian.' A more unhappy racing experience took place when the suffragette Emily Davison threw herself in front of the King's horse during the running of the Derby in 1913. She touched a rein and unseated the jockey; badly trampled, she died four days later from her injuries.

George did not immediately take over the Sandringham kennels after his father's death. He understood the pleasure Queen Alexandra took in all the dogs she kept there: a diversity of rare breeds, many of whom required special diets and attention. Earlier Edward VII had added a range of kennels for his gun dogs. These consisted of fourteen self-contained units, each with an enclosed run. When George succeeded to his father's throne most of his gun dogs were at first looked after by individual keepers in their own homes.

Although built long ago, the kennels have been kept up to date by Elizabeth II and are run on modern lines. There is a large paddock for exercising and – as in the days of the punctilious George V – every-

The King, out for an early morning ride in the Row in Hyde Park.

George V with Queen Mary in a carriage with a matched pair of greys, en route to Craithie Church. Today, the Queen and her family go by car when taking the same road from Balmoral.

thing is done to schedule. The dogs have their first meal at 6.30 a.m. and their evening meal at 4 p.m. Their exercise and grooming are carried out under the direction of skilled kennelmen, and their food is prepared in a spotless modern kitchen. As an energetic sportsman, George was much concerned about the working qualities of his dogs. During the shooting season they were expected to stand up to four or five days' work a week, and by royal command were always fed on raw meat.

The gun dogs first used by George V were the Clumber spaniels which his father had introduced to Sandringham. 'A Clumber,' Edward once said, 'can do the work of three beaters.' The most solid of the spaniel breed, they are heavily built with a solemn expression. Slow but thorough workers, they were well suited to the conditions at Sandringham at the time, and could track through the acres of bracken in which a bird can run for long distances without being seen.

Later, when the estate was replanted with tall-growing trees and coverts which encouraged the game birds to fly higher and thus enjoy a more sporting chance, George introduced the famous labrador retrievers to Sandringham. As one of the six best shots in England he took pride in bagging the elusive woodcock. Erratic in flight, they require a high degree of skill to bring them down.

Since his mother used 'Sandringham' as her prefix when registering the names of her dogs, King George used 'Wolferton' – the name of the local village and railway station – for his dogs while Alexandra was still alive. He took a keen interest in how his dogs fared at shows. His labrador Wolferton Jet, for which a breeder once offered £150 (which was refused), won many prizes at shows, including Crufts. Wolferton Ben, another labrador, won six Kennel Club challenge certificates. In later years, the best of George's labradors was Sandringham Stow, who won two first prizes and three seconds at the Crufts of 1932. In 1934 the King entered a team of four Clumbers and won the championship with a dog called Sandringham Spark. Born in 1928, Spark was quite the best-known Clumber of his day. When he died, only a couple of years after his big Crufts win, George grieved deeply.

Fortunately, all King George's other close pets seemed to live to a good age. He had a collie called Heather which was a close companion for eleven years, succeeded by a terrier named Happy which lived for thirteen years and Jack, a sealyham which died in 1928 at the age of fourteen. Their gravestones have been built into the wall of York Cottage stables at Sandringham. Each stone bears a tribute to 'the constant and faithful companion of His Majesty'.

Bob was a favourite name for the King's dogs. Sandringham Bob was the famous son of Sandringham Serum; both were prize-winning labrador retrievers bred at Sandringham during the thirties. But most famous of all was Bob the cairn terrier, owned by the King in his later years. This Bob would follow at the heels of his master's white pony Jock as they toured the estate together. Though small and not exactly a Crufts specimen, he was the King's most affectionate dog. He pined so much the first time the King left for Balmoral without him that thereafter he was always included in the royal party.

Of all the King's pets, Charlotte the parrot was the longest-lived. Appearing punctually each morning with Charlotte on his finger, he would allow her the freedom of the breakfast table. If the bird made a mess, the King would slide a mustard pot over it so that the Queen should not see. A distinguished guest once complained when she dug her beak into his boiled egg, but to visiting children Charlotte was a never-ending delight as she picked her way through the breakfast courses. Nor was the parrot forgotten when the King was away. Cruising in the Mediterranean, he wrote: 'Glad Charlotte is all right and that the housemaid is taking care of her.' Unlike the game-birds that he shot in their thousands, the King, like his mother, was devoted to pet birds and loved to visit the budgerigars and 'rare breeds from the Empire' that inhabited the aviary built by Alexandra at Sandringham.

With the people he knew and loved best, George was often a great tease. His chief gamekeeper, Bland, was highly efficient; but, as the

Above, *King George V and Queen Mary at Sandringham, standing beside a basket of racing pigeons. Originally of Belgian breed, the pigeons have broken several racing records and saved airmen in World War II.*

Left, *In full ceremonial, George V and his cousin Kaiser Wilhelm II at Potsdam in 1913. 'How are the mighty fallen' wrote the King on hearing that the Kaiser had abdicated in 1918.*

Left, *The future George V as Duke of York in 1905 on his moor pony, out shooting. Now the royal family use Range Rovers when travelling the moors.*
Right, *Thought to be little interested in animals, Princess May of Teck, wrote 'Georgie' (her future husband George V), several enthusiastic letters about her pet dog.*

Duke of Westminster once wrote, 'his approach was as solemn and grave as that of an ambassador presenting his letters of credence'. As soon as he arrived from London, the King would summon Bland and subject him to his own particular line of banter: 'Well, Bland, all the partridges drowned, I suppose?' Going round the estate, he would doff his hat and bid good morning to cottagers in a voice that could be heard half a mile away. Once, when he was out walking with his sister Maud, Queen of Norway, he noticed that she kept a special handkerchief for her little spaniel. Throughout the rest of the walk he kept up a running commentary: 'Where are its galoshes?' and 'Don't forget its cough drops'!

Although a formidable figure to his sons, especially his heir – the errant David, later Duke of Windsor, whom he constantly criticized – he was a loving father to his only daughter, Princess Mary. He indulged her love for horses with a succession of expensive ponies. Later, he was more forthcoming with his grandchildren than he had ever been with his own family, and there is a delightful story of the present Queen as a child playing horses and leading her grandfather by the beard as he shuffled along the floor on all fours.

Although Princess May, before she became Queen Mary, had owned a favourite hound and a carriage horse, it is often assumed that she showed little enthusiasm for dogs and horses. But as in everything during their years of marriage, she shared her husband's interests to the full. Whether going on walks with his dogs, accompanying him to see his racehorses compete, applauding when working his gun dogs or even humouring the parrot Charlotte, Queen Mary put her husband first in all things.

As a young woman, Princess May had been at a disadvantage on the marriage market. Although she was a descendant of George III, a morganatic marriage contracted by her grandfather was enough to disqualify her from making a match with a European reigning house. Nor did she possess a dowry. Her parents, the profligate Duke and Duchess of Teck, had, to use May's own words, been in 'Short Street' for many a long year.

Lacking the brilliant looks of her future mother-in-law Queen Alexandra, Princess May nevertheless possessed a sincerity and strength of character which greatly appealed to Queen Victoria. Discounting the many drawbacks, Victoria decided that she would make an eminently suitable bride for the heir apparent – Prince Eddy, Duke of Clarence and Avondale. A weak and wayward character, Eddy might well have turned out to be a disaster both as king and

George at Sandringham in 1902 with his four children. L to R:
Prince Albert, Princess Mary, Prince Edward, and Prince Henry,
standing in front of Caesar, King Edward VII's terrier.

*Winter at Sandringham with Edward VII seated resplendently at
the wheel of an early automobile. Next to his mother Queen Alexandra,
Prince George wears his dog's lead on his arm like a bracelet.*

husband; as it was, he died from pneumonia in 1892. With the royal
family plunged into mourning, May was virtually cast in the role of a
widow before she had become a wife. It was the future Edward VII who
decided that she would make a steady and amiable wife for his second
son, George.

Eighteen months after Eddy's death, Prince George, then Duke of
York, proposed and was accepted. Somewhat unromantically, the
proposal took place beside a frog pond in the garden of Sheen Lodge in
Richmond Park, the home of George's sister Princess Louise. But
whatever the circumstances, May proved an excellent wife to the
future sovereign and the marriage was a deeply happy one. Neither
was outwardly demonstrative, but the bond grew strong with time.
'You say you were proud of being my wife, I repeat that I was very
proud of being your husband', wrote George after their visit to the
Delhi Durbar nearly twenty years after their marriage.

During this state visit to India in 1912, when they were crowned
Emperor and Empress in Delhi, Queen Mary had an opportunity to
display her imperturbable character. After the exhausting pageantry
of the Durbar, King George had arranged to travel six hundred miles
for a big game shoot at the invitation of the Maharajah of Nepal.
Although such a thing would be frowned on today when preserving
wildlife is a priority, at that time tigers were more plentiful and tiger
shoots were the envied sport of maharajahs. The King's host had
excelled himself by providing several hundred elephants and over
fourteen hundred beaters for his hunt. Meanwhile, hundreds of miles
away, Queen Mary, who had independently travelled to view

Princess May of Teck, the future Queen Mary, with the pony and trap given to her as a 21st birthday present by the people of Richmond.

architectural splendours but was also taken to a tiger hunt, was seated in a tree hut crocheting when suddenly a tiger approached without warning. 'Look, Lord Shaftesbury – a tiger!' she called to the Lord Steward of the Royal Household, who was also present.

'I saw the tiger beautifully 40 yards away coming towards us,' she later wrote in her diary, 'but Ld Shaftesbury had his back to him.' Fortunately, the Queen instinctively did the right thing when faced defenceless by a tiger. As it stood staring at her, she steadily returned its gaze. After a few minutes it sprang silently away.

Like many people who do not have dogs of their own, Queen Mary took a keen interest in those belonging to her friends. During World War II she lived for a period at Badminton, home of the Duke and Duchess of Beaufort. Her niece, the Duchess, kept several dogs and, according to the royal biographer Kenneth Rose, the Queen would ceremoniously give one particular pet a dog biscuit every night after dinner. One night when the local bishop came to dine, she thought to delegate the nightly ritual to him, handing him the biscuit with a few words of explanation. As it happened, the bishop was rather hard of hearing and thought he was being presented with a special delicacy. As he proceeded to munch the biscuit to the last crumb, Queen Mary sat immobilized, daring anyone to laugh until he had left the room.

The aunt of the present Aga Khan discovered a lighter side to Queen Mary's imposing character when she visited a house where the now-widowed Queen was a frequent guest. On one occasion when the Queen was there, visiting the former Prime Minister Arthur Balfour and his wife, she found her hosts surrounded by a multitude of dogs. Queen Mary's attention was immediately caught by one entrancing puppy which had lagged behind its mother. Picking it up, she pressed it to her bosom and nuzzled her face in its fur. At that precise moment the puppy spent a penny.

The front of Queen Mary's gown was soaked, but, far from being put out, she laughed heartily, passing the whole incident off as a joke at her own expense. To show that there were no hard feelings, she called her hostess to bring a camera and insisted on being photographed with the only puppy known to have wet the Queen.

It was while inspecting troops in France during World War I that George suffered a cruel accident. Having arrived behind the lines, he was provided with a fine-looking chestnut horse. But, riding towards a loudly cheering detachment of the Royal Flying Corps, the apparently docile charger suddenly reared up like a rocket and came over backwards on top of the King.

In his memoirs, *Horseman*, Captain J. H. Marshall tells how he was asked to produce a quality horse for His Majesty's visit during some of the worst fighting of the war. He was in charge of a horse depot near Le Havre when a general came to make a selection. Marshall told him: 'It would be wiser to put His Majesty up on something that's already in or near the line and is used to shells and mortars, whizz bangs, barbed wire and all the rest.' He was understandably unhappy when the general chose a young Irish horse that Marshall considered quite unsuitable for the Front.

The night after the accident the King was in agony. The doctors who were called to examine him failed to detect the extent of his injuries, which included a fractured pelvis. But despite the intense pain and shock he insisted on decorating a sergeant of the Coldstream Guards with the Victoria Cross before departing for a rough sea crossing home. Back in London he made a slow recovery, and suffered pain from the injury for the remaining twenty years or so of his life.

As he grew older, George's happiest hours were still those spent at Sandringham, where he loved to be but where he was to die. The Christmas of 1935 was bitterly cold. The King's health was failing and, although unable to hold a gun, he still rode out on his pony Jock, taking the usual carrot in his pocket. With Queen Mary and his granddaughter, the nine-year-old Princess Elizabeth – the future Elizabeth II – at his side, he saw the snow powdering the Norfolk countryside for the last time.

By mid-January the King had succumbed to a rapid decline. Members of the Privy Council, including the Prime Minister, came down to Sandringham to receive his last signature. Assembled in the sitting room which led to the King's bedroom, they found Charlotte the parrot

Above, *Princess Mary, the Princess Royal with a King penguin at London Zoo in 1911. Her father had become King thirteen months earlier.*

Left, *Princess Mary, only daughter of George V, with pet Pomeranian at their modest family home, York Cottage on the Sandringham estate.*

moping in a corner. After his death the King's coffin, made of oak from a tree grown on the Sandringham estate, rested for a time at the local church. Following immediately behind the coffin on the way to Wolferton station, from where the King was to be taken back to London for a state funeral, was Jock, led by a groom. Later, his eldest son – briefly to become Edward VIII – wrote: 'Just as we topped the last hill above the station the stillness of the morning was broken by a wild and familiar sound – the crow of a cock pheasant.'

4

THE WINDSORS

'In the hunting field I could forget
my round of duties.'

'Why doesn't my son ride like a gentleman?' demanded King George V
of Captain 'Fruity' Metcalfe, equerry to the Prince of Wales.

'Because he does not have Your Majesty's hands,' came the
diplomatic reply.

The King had observed that the Prince used a snaffle when out
steeplechasing, but the absence of the more conventional double bridle
was by no means the monarch's only complaint against his eldest son
Edward, known to family and friends as David. Family life was always
difficult for the heir to the throne.

In his autobiography, *A King's Story*, the then Duke of Windsor
wrote about how he had enjoyed riding with his brothers and sister
when they were children at Sandringham. 'The happiest hours were
those in which we three [boys] were left to our own resources. Mary
was our close companion in many of our activities. . . . Mary could at
times be quite a "Tomboy"; but at others, supported by her formidable
"Mademoiselle", she wielded a sweet tyranny over our lives.' At six
Mary had been given a donkey called Ben. She adored him, and only
slowly transferred her affections to the ponies and horses which were
to become her lifelong hobby.

Apparently young David had a fine relationship with his grandfather, Edward VII, who was not averse to using the boy to help him
carry out a little joke. One day David was at Balmoral at the same time
as Sir Felix Semon, the King's physician. Semon had unhappily
managed to kill a stag that was undersize. At a shooting lunch a few
days later, the Prince was prompted to go up to Semon and ask: 'Have
you killed a little staggie today, Sir Felix?'

'Who set you up to this, Prince Eddie?' the doctor asked.

Truthfully – and ingenuously – the boy replied: 'Grandpapa.'

Unfortunately, his relationship with his father was never as good as
the one with his grandfather. By 1911, when David was Prince of
Wales and his father now George V, he spent a winter at Sandringham
while his parents went to India. At Sandringham he was expected to
prepare himself for going up to Oxford. He wrote to his father,
thanking him for permitting him to shoot at Sandringham, and said
how much he loved shooting. 'I have had some splendid practice, & feel
that my shooting has much improved. It is the small days that give one

*Edward, Prince of Wales, at Fort Belvedere with Cora and Jaggs,
first of the Cairn terriers. He gave Cairn puppies to two of the
women he loved: Freda Dudley Ward and Wallis Simpson.*

far more practice than the big ones. One can take one's time and shoot
much better.' (Small days in shooting circles refer to those when 'guns'
go over coverts known to have fewer game.)

Back came the King's reply from HMS *Medina*, returning from
India:

> Judging from your letters and from the number of days you have been
> shooting, there can't be much game left at Sandringham, I should think. It
> also seems a mistake to shoot the coverts three times over, I never do that
> unless a few more cocks have to be killed. . . . You seem to be having too
> much shooting and not enough riding or hunting. You must learn to ride
> and hunt properly. . . . I must say I am disappointed.

Although George V himself was an excellent shot, he only encouraged his son to ride, not to shoot. Later, when he was Duke of Windsor,
David remembered how in several of his father's early letters he was
pressed to improve his horsemanship: 'In your position it is absolutely
necessary that you should ride well as you will continually have to do
so at parades, reviews, etc., and so the sooner you make up your mind
to the better. The English people like riding and it would make you

Edward was a fearless rider, though not an especially polished one. Fears about the future King's safety increased during the 1920s and after a heavy fall at an Army point-to-point, his parents stopped him from steeplechasing.

very unpopular if you couldn't do so. If you can't ride, you know, I am afraid people will call you a duffer.'

In 1912, when an opportunity arose to send the Prince of Wales to Paris, off he went. He rode in the Bois de Boulogne, played golf – he had been caddying for his father and for his grandfather for several years – and was taken to the magnificent local racecourses, Longchamp and Auteuil.

Back in England, now at Oxford, Edward began complaining that riding was dull. King George then sent him Major the Hon. William Cadogan as equerry. Cadogan not only managed to improve his skill but fired in him a new enthusiasm for various kinds of horsemanship. Subsequently Prince Edward hunted with the South Oxfordshire Hounds and began playing polo. There was a precedent for the polo: his father's late elder brother – the Duke of Clarence and Avonmore – was exceptionally keen on the sport.

Now came a different tone from George V. 'You certainly have been doing a great deal; hunting two days, out with the beagles twice, golf and shooting one day, besides all your work, which seems a good deal for one week. I only hope you are not overdoing it in the way of exercise.' There seemed no pleasing his stern, disciplinarian father.

In 1914 war broke out, and in November that year Prince Edward had joined the army. He had already spent part of two Junes in the summer camp of the Oxford Battalion of the Officers' Training Corps, and in July 1914 he had gone to the 1st Life Guards. His father still felt

*By 1935, marriage to Wallis had become Edward's fixed intention.
When she couldn't be with him, the prince kept Slipper for company.*

determined that his son should have a better 'seat' on a horse, and
hoped that parading in a riding school with a riding master would do
the trick.

After the war, he began to ride in point-to-points. His first was the
Grenadier Guards Race at Warden Hill, in which he rode a horse called
Pet Dog. He came in third, in a field of sixteen, which is rather amazing
considering he had fallen at the second fence and had then remounted
and rejoined the field. Next he won the Pytchley Hunt point-to-point,
this time on a good horse called Rifle Grenade; he led by five lengths
over the last fence and won by a length. In all he won six races, was
second five times, and third once. In order to be near his horses he
leased a house called Euston Gray in the Beaufort country, and later
rooms at Craven Lodge in Melton Mowbrey, where the famous horse
painter Sir Alfred Munnings loved to work.

'Although I was taught to ride as a small boy, and had done a little
fox-hunting at Oxford,' he wrote in *A King's Story*,

> I did not take it up seriously until 1920–21, when I began to hunt with the
> Pytchley in Northamptonshire. . . . Hunting and steeplechasing were more
> than exhilarating exercise to me. In the hunting field I could forget my
> round of duties. I was too busy riding my horse and scanning the next fence
> for a place to jump to worry over my next engagement or my next
> speech. . . . There is no thrill to equal that of riding a good, keen horse. . . .
> Just as my father was one of the best shots in the country, so it was my
> ambition to be a good rider to hounds.

But the King was not pleased with his son. He addressed himself to the Queen: 'Yesterday David had a fall riding in a point-to-point race near Aldershot and bruised and cut his face a little and got a slight concussion, but it is nothing serious. . . . It is too bad that he should continue to ride in these steeple chases. I have asked him not to on many occasions. . . .'

When George V became gravely ill in 1929, Queen Mary asked her son to give up point-to-points and steeplechasing and be content just with riding. But the Prince of Wales was a man of extremes. He sold all his horses and gave up his rooms at Craven Lodge; deprived by emotional blackmail of the thrill of steeplechasing, he gave up hunting too. Dogs, however, remained an enthusiasm, as they would to the end of his life.

During the war the Prince had begun his long series of affairs with married women. The last of these, and the one that was to lead to his abdication, was with the American Wallis Simpson. She rapidly took over the running of Fort Belvedere, the Prince's house in Surrey, which shocked many members of the Prince's circle who were used to greater discretion from the various royal mistresses. However, his closest companion at the Fort – a Jack Russell terrier – accepted Wallis. She had a clever way with dogs that was tied in with the commanding-demanding-pandering style that had entranced the Prince. One moment she scolded and slapped, the next she caressed.

In *The Heart Has Its Reasons*, the Duchess of Windsor's memoirs published in 1956, she talked about the origins of a favourite little cairn terrier called Slipper (also known as Mr Loo because of his untidy toilet habits). 'Part of my affection for the Fort extended to the Prince's cairns Cora and Jaggs,' she wrote. 'Unknown to me the Prince had observed the growth of our friendship. One afternoon he turned up at Bryanston Court [a block of London flats where she then lived] with a cairn puppy under his arm. "This", he said, "is Slipper. He is yours."'

By 1935 Edward and Wallis had developed a private language of their own, with Slipper as their secret bond. Joining Cora and Jaggs at the Fort for little holidays, Slipper kept the Prince company when parted from Wallis. 'The babies send you . . . flowers', he wrote to her. 'Mr Loo and I are up here in our blue room and missing you like the dickens.'

Christmas 1935 saw Slipper at Sandringham. The Prince could hardly bear to part from Wallis and Slipper was his only consolation. He found the strain at Sandringham intolerable. 'The worst Christmas I have ever had to spend with the family, far worse than last year and that was bad enough,' he wrote later. Edward had hoped to discuss the matters weighing on his mind: the possibility of his future marriage to the woman whom his parents refused to receive in their own

Above, *Fed from silver bowls, the Windsors regarded their family of pugs as substitute children. Lady Diana Cooper gave them their first pair of pugs and commented, 'very soon the pugs weren't their pugs any more: they were her pugs.'*

Left, *In the hunting field, Edward went 'like a bomb' according to those who rode with him. Top hats were the fashion at this meet of the Beaufort Hunt in 1923, but offered little protection against injury.*

home; the woman he now loved 'madly, tenderly and adoringly'. But he and his father were frozen in a state of misunderstanding, and the time and place for that discussion were never to come.

After George V died in February 1936, Edward and Wallis, together with Slipper as a third member of the unofficial family, began a round of visiting. The widowed Queen Mary was not amused by the reports she heard, especially by accounts of Wallis's visit to Balmoral where she took over the reins of the household and Slipper slept on the royal beds.

But it was rapidly becoming clear that the new King could not have both the crown and a divorced American commoner as his wife. After much soul-searching, he made the agonizing decision to abdicate in favour of his next brother, who was to become George VI. Now to be known as the Duke of Windsor, be decided to leave England for ever and go to live abroad.

Even on the fateful day of the Abdication broadcast Edward found time to think about Slipper, whom Wallis, who had already gone abroad to await the completion of her divorce from Ernest Simpson, had left behind at Fort Belvedere. In *A King's Story* he wrote:

> The moment had come to leave the Fort for good. My bags were packed. In the act of bidding farewell to the small group of personal retainers gathered in the hall, I discovered Slipper at my heels. In the commotion of packing he was obviously worried that he would be left behind. Patting the little dog to reassure him, I said, 'Of course you are coming away with me, Slipper. But you can't come to this family dinner-party.' And turning to [the statesman] Walter Monckton, I said, 'Be sure to bring Slipper with you in the car when you come to fetch me for the broadcast.'

While he and Wallis were separated – so that there could be no accusations of collusion in the matter of her divorce – their letters to each other always contained news and inquiries about Slipper. 'He looks very well and has a lovely time on the golf course in the afternoon, then eats an enormous dinner followed by Bob Martin's [conditioning tablets] every 2 or 3 evenings,' wrote the Duke. Wallis in return sent 'a pat to Slipey Poo'.

Wallis ended up at the Château de Candé, near Tours, which had been lent by their friend Charles Bedaux, an American industralist, and where they were eventually to be married. Here she took charge of Slipper again, who arrived with messages from the Duke, plus all his essential accoutrements including brush, comb, English dog biscuits, Bob Martin's tablets and his own special rug. Only when he bounded into her arms did Wallis feel that the long and troubled vigil which had separated her from David might at last have a happy ending.

But in the first week of April 1937, six weeks before the wedding was to take place, tragedy struck. Wallis was out walking on the golf

In 1956, the dogs won prizes at the International Canine Exhibition in Paris. The Duke is seen with Goldengleam Trooper who gained a second, and the Duchess with Davy Crockett who came first.

course with Slipper when he was bitten by a snake. The poison reached his heart before she could get him to the vet. 'Now the principal guest at our wedding is no more,' wrote an anguished Wallis to David. 'He was our dog – not yours or mine but ours and he loved us both so.'

The letters of Wallis and Edward, edited by Michael Bloch, make it clear how overwhelmed both were by the loss of the pet who had been so faithful through all their travails. 'Oh, how utterly cruel that our darling Mr Loo should be taken from WE like this,' wrote the Duke. 'My heart is quite breaking this morning my beloved sweetheart. . . .' A diamond-encrusted slipper embedded in a medallion, inscribed 'Our Mr Loo', was commissioned in memory of the little dog. Later it was kept in pride of place in the Windsors' house in the Bois de Boulogne.

They were not, however, without canine company for long. When

Slipper had been sent to Wallis in France, the Duke, unable to exist without a dog for even a few weeks, had promptly bought a new cairn puppy. He had called the new addition Schnuki, but Wallis had renamed it Pookie. Now, on hearing the sad news about Slipper, Charles Bedaux's wife bought them yet another cairn, which they called Preezie. It was a kind gesture, but nothing could fill the emotional void left by the little cairn's death. 'The new dog is sweet,' wrote Wallis to her Aunt Bessie in America, 'but he is not Slipper.'

The long-awaited wedding took place at the Château de Candé on 3 June 1937. No member of the royal family attended the ceremony, and with the absence of the little dog who had meant so much to them there was a shadow over the day.

Naturally, however, as dog lovers, they grew to love the newcomers. The only trace of their occupation of a Riviera villa which they rented after the war is a grave marked 'Preezie'. The inscription reads: 'A Faithful Little Friend of Edward and Wallis, Duke and Duchess of Windsor – 1937–49.' Indeed, when later they sold their mill house in the French countryside, they insisted on a clause protecting the graves of their dogs. But no dog ever totally replaced Slipper, and when the last of the cairns died in the early 1950s it was the end of the dynasty.

The cairns gave way to pugs. According to Lady Diana Cooper, in a personal account given to this author, she had been the first person to give dogs of this breed to the Windsors. 'I gave them to *him*, you know. But before you knew what happened, they were *her* pugs.' Wallis's possessiveness did not make her universally popular among Edward's circle.

There were several contradictory aspects to her character. She purported to love animals, but on at least one occasion she made a scene when disturbed by a furry pet. The first recorded incident happened in the summer of 1934, when she accompanied the Prince of Wales abroad. She told the story herself in her autobiography.

> Posy, as we called her, was an old friend. . . . She was a cousin by marriage of Lord Moyne, son of Lord Iveagh, of the famous Guinness brewing family. Lord Moyne . . . was cruising nearby in his yacht, *Rosaura*. Posy suggested that it might be fun to take a cruise with him. . . . Having by now had enough of Biarritz, the Prince jumped at the idea. . . . As a matter of fact it was blowing a full gale. . . . So far as I was concerned the final straw was supplied by the untimely incursion of Lord Moyne's pet, a terrifying monkey that had the run of the vessel. Just when I had decided that I had endured all I could bear, there was a scrabbling and chattering in the skylight over my head. A moment later, a furry, twisting object hurtled down, landing on the foot of my bed. Then I let out a scream that must have carried to Lord Moyne on the bridge: for a steward came rushing in. After one look he beat a hasty retreat. Finally a sailor who had the monkey's confidence appeared and coaxed him away.

Black Diamond was the last of the Windsor pugs. He remained on his master's bed during his last illness, but on the final day jumped to the floor, alerting the ex-king's physician that the last hour was near.

That cruise was not all disaster. She wrote: 'Perhaps it was during these evenings off the Spanish coast that we crossed the line that marks the indefinable boundary between friendship and love.' Love, she did feel. It was probably greater at that time, and waned for her with the passing years. Partly at fault was the fact that the Duke of Windsor never managed to make the royal family agree to give her the title of Her Royal Highness.

Life in exile, remembering a throne that might have been Edward's, cannot have been easy. He longed to serve his country in some capacity, but the nearest he got was the undemanding post of Governor-General of the Bahamas. They were both accustomed to a life of luxury, with fine houses and furnishings, *couture* clothes for Wallis, and entertaining on a lavish scale. But as an ex-king Edward had forfeited some of his claims to royal funds, and the Windsors often had money problems. When, just after the Abdication, a friend asked him whether he would continue racing as an owner, he replied sadly: 'I'm too poor to own horses.' The Duke and Duchess lived mostly in France, but spent time in various other countries, including visits to Hitler and Franco which were, perhaps, politically naive. Wherever they went, they had canine companionship.

In Paris the dogs lived in as grand a style as their owners, and were said to be accorded greater respect than the Windsors' guests. The dogs ate out of silver dishes, and their leads were woven from silver and gold thread. David felt very happy to have a home where his dogs could reign, even if he no longer could.

The curious little family of pugs which shared the Windsors' years of exile numbered nine in all: after the heartbreak of Slipper it may have seemed safer to keep dogs in numbers. The first generation were named Trooper, Disraeli, Imp and Davy Crockett, and were doted on like substitute children. 'Naughty boy!' Wallis would scold as Disraeli scrambled over a silken sofa. When guests arrived, wrote Suzy Menkes in *The Windsor Style*, 'the dogs ran wild before dinner, like children brought down from the nursery to show themselves off'.

Sleek and shiny and pale beige in colour, the first generation of pugs blended almost like a fashion accessory with many of the chic Duchess's Dior outfits. In 1956 they won prizes at the International Canine Exhibition in Paris. The Duke was pictured with Goldengleam Trooper who gained a second, and the Duchess with Davy Crockett who won a first.

Pugs were a recurrent image at the Windsors' Paris house, reproduced in paintings, sculptures and a famous collection of eighteenth-century Meissen figurines. At night the real ones were laid out on a plastic cover on the Duchess's bed; and on a bedroom sofa, each had a pug-shaped pillow. A playful breed, the pugs would snuffle and romp around as the Duke talked to them and tended his English garden at the Moulin de la Tuilerie.

The Windsors spent four months of the year in America, and would usually bring their dogs with them. 'The Duchess was a fantastic house guest,' remembers a friend. 'When they used to stay with my mother-in-law in Long Island, she would bring her four dogs. They weren't always totally house-trained, but she trained her staff to clear up after them.' They continued to travel with their pets even in extreme old age.

In 1972, on his deathbed, the Duke clung to a pug called Black Diamond. A French physician who attended him noted that every time he visited his patient the dog was on the bed. But on the last day Black Diamond came down to sit alone on the carpet. By dawn the Duke was dead.

5

GEORGE VI, QUEEN ELIZABETH AND THE LITTLE PRINCESSES

'Perhaps I can help.
I am rather good with dogs.'

On a cheerless night a fortnight before the Christmas of 1936, HMS *Fury* left Portsmouth harbour with the eldest son of King George V aboard. The to be named HRH The Duke of Windsor had abdicated after eleven months as Edward VIII. It was to be the fate of his brother Albert Frederick Arthur George, known like his grandfather Edward VII as Bertie, to succeed to a throne he had never wanted and to spend a large part of his reign in the throes of a devastating war and its aftermath.

The Abdication crisis had left him little time to attend to the traditional sport of kings. All the same, within a week of his accession George VI had made it clear that he intended to continue with the royal stables and stud, and those racehorses which the departing Edward VIII had leased to Lord Derby during his brief reign. 'I shall certainly take a great interest in racing,' George wrote in characteristically modest style to his racing manager, 'but of course at the moment I know nothing about breeding or anything else so you must teach me.'

The new monarch was to find that the stables were not the only royal institution to have reached a low ebb. Sandringham had been uninhabited since the death of his father, and Buckingham Palace needed modernization. So it was a great boost when Jubilee, bred by George V, won the Molyneaux Stakes at Liverpool a year later. Two days afterwards Bertie, accompanied by the Queen, was thrilled to see his horse Royal Mail win the Grand National. It was an encouraging start.

Pitchforked into a new life of public responsibility, Bertie was forty-one and Elizabeth thirty-six when the small and youthful family group found themselves in charge at Sandringham for Christmas. Princess Elizabeth, then ten, and the six-year-old Princess Margaret Rose set about exploring. They started with the coach house, and the royal biographer Helen Cathcart writes how delighted they were with some extraordinary finds including a Japanese rickshaw, two ancient Norwegian carriages, the Hungarian victoria from Budapest once driven by Queen Alexandra, and an immense padded charabanc which

Bertie was taught the correct way to ride. As Duke of York, he hunted with the Pytchley and the Quorn and as King George VI, his racehorses had many classic wins.

had belonged to the Emperor Napoleon III. A saddle room contained even more exciting treasures: a splendid set of Indian harness, the great jockey Fred Archer's racing saddle, and a Mexican saddle with lasso that had once been presented to Buffalo Bill.

The children's enthusiasm fired their father to remember that even the unreadiest of Kings should have some relaxations. He bought a new game book to record the duck-shooting, and became so fascinated by wildfowling that he later recorded that he had spent four hours in a hide in a kale field waiting for the birds to fly over. Like his father, he might have succumbed to the serenity of Sandringham had not the rush of coronation year, followed by the warnings of Hitler's aggression in Europe, not made his presence in London an ever-increasing necessity.

With the declaration of war, Sandringham was seldom used. Lawns were ploughed up to yield oats and rye; beetroots, parsnips, peas and beans were grown in the flower beds by Land Girls; and troops were billeted at York Cottage.

It seems strange that horse-racing continued throughout the war

Animals were a natural part of life to the Bowes-Lyon family. At the age of 9, Elizabeth was riding side-saddle on Bobs, the Shetland pony.

years. But, along with theatres and cinemas, race meetings were considered a morale-boosting relaxation, enjoyed both by civilians and by troops on leave. So when in 1942 the King won the triple crown (the One Thousand Guineas, the Oaks and the St Leger) with his horse Sun Chariot, Britain's sports-minded public felt they had something to celebrate. Both Sun Chariot and Big Game, which subsequently won the Two Thousand Guineas, had been leased to the King by the National Stud. They proved to be two of the best racehorses ever to have carried royal colours; and, because of their public ownership, racegoers felt they had a share in their monarch's victories.

George VI was also fond of his piggery at Sandringham, and visited it often. In common with his wartime Prime Minister, Winston Churchill, he may have felt that 'Dogs look up to us. Cats look down on us. Pigs treat us as equals.' Certainly he loved domesticity and country life.

Like his elder brother, Bertie had had a childhood long on discipline and short on affection. Several minor disabilities – a stutter, knock

Elizabeth was twenty-two when she accepted Bertie's proposal.
When the cameras came out, two cairns and a couple of labrador
puppies had to be included in the picture.

knees, and teeth which needed a brace – contributed to a marked
nervous temperament. All these disadvantages played a role – so
modern research would have us believe – in bringing about the cancer
which was to cause his death in early middle age. His parents were not
unloving, but, according to the custom of their class and generation,
believed in handing their children totally into the care of others. As a
small child, Bertie had suffered from the tyrannies of an unbalanced
nurse, who – while cherishing his brother David – had starved him in
the cradle and undermined the foundations of his health. This had
been followed by the supervision of a tutor who had forced the left-
handed Prince to use his right hand.

Yet in rising to the challenge posed by his elder brother's abdication,
the apparently unsuitable Bertie possessed two outstanding advan-
tages. One was the decency and integrity of his own character. The
other was what David had described in his Abdication speech as 'the
matchless blessing of a happy marriage'.

Bertie's marriage to Lady Elizabeth Bowes Lyon in 1923 had formed
the cornerstone of his life. 'You will be a fortunate fellow if you manage
to carry her off,' George V had remarked astringently. But the Prince
had wooed and finally won her, after proposing at least three times.

The Duke and Duchess of York arriving at Glamis in 1925.
Elizabeth refused to be parted from her favourite dogs when she
married Bertie, and with her is Mimsy, the Golden Labrador.

The ninth child of the Earl of Strathmore had an irresistible charm combined with a sparkling personality which had already brought her five other proposals in one year. Her father lived the life of a cricket-playing squire, and the family divided their time between the ancient castle at Glamis in Scotland and the mellow, rambling comforts of their house at St Paul's Waldenbury in Hertfordshire.

In recalling her early memories of St Paul's, Elizabeth, now the Queen Mother, described a wood at the bottom of the garden where 'there are carpets of anenomes and primroses to sit on' and 'whenever a dead bird is found in this enchanted world it is given a solemn burial in a small box lined with rose leaves'. In the harness room, 'besides hens there are bantams . . . also Persian kittens and tortoises. . . .' There were always dogs, of several breeds; and ponies, which were passed down from one child to the next. Cats, farm animals and a selection of tame birds were equally cherished.

Appropriately, Bertie's successful proposal had been made when walking in the countryside at St Paul's Waldenbury. They had been visiting Bobs, Elizabeth's old Shetland pony on which she had learned to ride side-saddle. 'Her tastes are chiefly for an outdoor life. She rides and goes well to hounds, although she has not hunted nearly as much as she would have liked. . . .' This impression of Elizabeth at the time of her marriage to Bertie, then Duke of York, shows that she was fully in tune with her husband's interests from the first.

Later little more was heard of her hunting, but Elizabeth's unruffled temperament and talent for home-making proved to be the attributes which Bertie's affectionate nature had craved since boyhood. The future King could never have met the challenges which lay ahead without the bedrock of a happy family life in which dogs, horses and so many aspects of country life played an essential part. This became a pattern which has influenced the royal family's way of life ever since.

Although not spectacular at the crash-and-dash tactics which had distinguished his elder brother's performance at point-to-points, Bertie was regarded by many as being the most polished horseman among the royal Princes. After his marriage, he continued hunting with the Pytchley in Northamptonshire for several seasons. But, as with many things that happened to Bertie, fate decreed that troubles loomed ahead.

In 1931, Prime Minister Ramsay MacDonald's first National Government imposed an era of frugality. Bertie decided he would have to give up hunting and cut down on other expenses. Just how much this meant to the future King is shown in the letter he wrote to the Pytchley's Master of Foxhounds: 'It has come as a great shock to me that, with the economy cuts, I have had to make my hunting one of the things I must do without. And I must sell my horses too. This is the worst part of it all, and the parting with them will be terrible – the horses are looking so well too.'

He continued with the less expensive pastimes of tennis and golf. Like his father and grandfather, he also took part in the seasonal shooting of grouse, pheasant and partridge. But there was a new, over-riding passion – gardening. At Royal Lodge, Windsor, the Duke and Duchess of York had found an idyllic setting for family life.

It had not been lived in for a century, so the considerable improvements needed took a long time to achieve, but Royal Lodge was the Yorks' transformation scene. Both had missed having a garden of their own, and they set to with a will to landscape and plant the grounds, which by the time of George VI's death had increased from 15 to 90 acres.

Comfortable chintz chairs and flower-filled rooms gave the Yorks' new home an unpretentious country house atmosphere. Outside, the walls were painted in a pink wash. An aviary for sky-blue budgerigars provided a source of constant fascination for the growing Princesses. In the garden a bird table encouraged small birds to perch; they were rewarded with food when they rang a bell.

Born in 1926, Princess Elizabeth represented everything Bertie had aspired to in his own childhood. Lively, confident and inquiring,

Above, *On the day of her twelfth birthday, Princess Elizabeth was pictured riding her pony Greylight with Princess Margaret on the leading rein on Gem. To avoid jealousy, the King told the cameraman: 'In no circumstances is Princess Margaret to be left out of the picture.'*

Left, *The Duke and Duchess of York with the little Princesses, corgis Jane and Dookie, and Tibetan Lion Dog, Choo Choo. Soon after this picture was taken in the rose garden at Royal Lodge, Windsor, the Duke of York became King and all of their lives changed completely.*

Lilibet – as she nicknamed herself when she was unable to pronounce her full name – greeted each new day as a wonderful adventure. She was a small figure with a mop of fair curls when a new governess, Marion Crawford (soon to be known as Crawfie), joined the family. The Princess had just been given her first pony, Peggy, by her grandfather, George V. Sitting up in bed in the night nursery, Lilibet had tied the cords of her dressing-gown to the knobs of the old-fashioned bed and was busy driving a team of imaginary horses.

'Do you usually drive in bed?' Miss Crawford asked.

'I mostly go once or twice round the park before I go to sleep, you know,' she said. 'It exercises my horses.'

When she was six, the people of Wales gave her a model house. Fifteen feet high, it was thatched and had a chimney. There were blue chintz curtains at the windows, and it had a bathroom plus kitchen complete with running water. The little girls looked after it themselves, dusting and cleaning it. And they invited their pets in for tea.

As their daughters grew, so did the Yorks' collection of dogs. Some years back, the Duke had singled out Mimsy as his own special gun dog. A yellow labrador, Mimsy had become a family pet and had given birth to two puppies, Stiffy and Scrummy. They were a well-behaved threesome. At a word from their master, they would sit obediently in a row. Joining them was Choo-Choo, a long-haired Tibetan lion dog or Shih Tzu, meaning 'lion' in Chinese. Of a game and sporting disposition, Choo-Choo, given to the couple during their Empire tour, attached himself primarily to the Duchess. The name of Choo-Choo had been bestowed on him because, explained the Duke, 'when he first came to us as a puppy he made noises exactly like a train'. Also known as 'the animated dish cloth' or 'hairy monster', Choo-Choo had an oriental aloofness of character; and, no matter what business the other dogs were about, he kept his distance. Later, his grandson Ching came to live with the royal family, but the line of this breed died out during World War II.

Today the royal family is always associated with corgis, but back in the 1930s the breed was not at all well known. The Kennel Club, that august body which controls the breeding of pedigree dogs, did not admit the corgi as a breed worthy of championship status until 1928. Up until then the cocker spaniel, wire-haired terrier and Pekinese had been among the favourite pets of the British. The first Pembrokeshire corgi to hit the news was Dookie, whose picture appeared in the newspapers in 1933. The seven-year-old Princess Elizabeth was shown steering a strange-looking puppy over the steps of a railway bridge near Glamis Castle; thousands of people who saw the picture had never heard of a Welsh corgi before.

Macdonald Daly, a well-known dog judge of the era, relates in his book *Royal Dogs* how Mrs Thelma Gray – renowned for her cham-

Left: *The Windsors changed from beige to black pugs in the 1960s. The Duke and Duchess shown on arrival in New York with black pug, Minoroo, in 1966. The Duchess had previously flouted quarantine regulations, smuggling pet dogs into England illegally.*

Below: *Princess Anne, the Princess Royal, with her corgi Apollo and Dumfriesshire hound.*

Above: *HM The Queen visiting her mother's estate Birkhall, near Braemar, Scotland, accompanied by a bouquet of corgis.*

Right: *Prince Harry and his rabbit, held for him by an anxious parent who hopes that he will react as is best for the rabbit. One eye expresses the rabbit's emotion.*

Left: *HM The Queen and HRH The Duke of Edinburgh inspect a seal during a visit to the USA. HM The Queen has called for more efforts to keep the North Sea free of pollution. At a Windsor Castle banquet in honour of HM The King of Norway, she said, 'It is in the interests of both our nations to see that the health and cleanliness of the North Sea are maintained, and that its renewable resources are exploited only on a sustainable basis.' The Duke of Edinburgh is one of the world's foremost conservationists, working tirelessly to save endangered species, and to improve the habitat of those that are not.*

Right: *HRH Prince Michael of Kent cuddles a kitten. His family have tried several breeds, among them Siamese and Burmese.*

Above: *Prince and Princess Michael of Kent with their daughter Gabriella at home in Gloucestershire where they keep goats as well as an assortment of dogs and cats.*

Above: *Prince Charles with his friend Tigger.*

Left: *Prince Harry, during a trip to Spain as the guest of King Juan Carlos, rescued Queen Sophia's dog Bobby when he thought the canine was in trouble. Diana has brought her family up to have a respect for animals and to take a part in looking after their welfare.*

Right: *The Queen Mother pats the Irish Wolfhound mascot of a regiment on parade. This is the largest breed of canine in the British Isles.*

Above: Sarah has a great fear of snakes and shortly after meeting this feathered friend in Connecticut (autumn 1987), wept tears of terror when a huge python was produced.

Below: The Duchess was rather more amused when shown a giant tortoise wearing a Union Jack in Mauritius.

Princess Margaret at the reins with her sister, Elizabeth, as they drive through Windsor Great Park in 1940. Along for the ride is Jane, the corgi that ruled the roost for most of the war years.

pionship corgis – took three puppies up to the Yorks' London home at 145 Piccadilly for the Duke and his family to make a selection. Two of the puppies were tail-less, like most Welsh corgis of the Pembrokeshire breed, but one had a tiny stump of a tail. The Duchess came to a speedy decision. 'We must have the one which has something to wag,' she said. 'Otherwise, how are we going to know whether he is pleased or not?'

Selected for a royal future, Dookie first had to return to Surrey with Mrs Gray for a month's house training. During this time he got the name of Dookie because – according to Mrs Gray – he became so pleased with himself that he refused to eat from the same dish as the other puppies. Accordingly he was called the Duke, which in due course was shortened to Dookie. Explaining all this to the Duke of York caused Mrs Gray some embarrassment, as it was obvious that there was nothing in the least snooty about the real Duke.

Apart from making the corgi breed famous, Dookie had a proud ancestry. His father had been Crymmych President, a champion of the show ring. And his half brother Rozavel Red Dragon, who lived to the extraordinary age of seventeen, won even more prizes.

Like most corgis, Dookie was wonderfully healthy, active and hardy, and a great success with the children. Corgis can be trained for almost anything at an early age, and he proved an inspirational playmate. But despite his distinguished breeding, Dookie – whose kennel name was Rozavel Golden Eagle – was not destined to found a dynasty. Unfortunately, he had no interest whatsoever in the opposite sex.

When Princess Margaret wanted a dog of her own it was decided to provide her with another corgi, Rozavel Lady Jane. The intention was to mate her with Dookie; but, as sometimes happens when dogs are constant companions, romance refused to blossom. A new marriage was then arranged for Jane, who was mated with Tafferteffy, the sire of numerous winners and as pure-bred a Pembrokeshire corgi as could be found.

Great was the excitement on Christmas Eve 1938 when Jane gave birth to a litter of puppies. The children had their choice and kept two, who were given the seasonal names of Crackers and Carol. Thus was the royal corgi dynasty founded; and since that day neither the Queen nor the Queen Mother has ever been without a Welsh corgi as a devoted companion.

If Dookie's nose was somewhat out of joint over this happy event, he was not left in the shade. The new King George VI paid him a gracious tribute: 'He really is the greatest personality of a dog I have ever known. So intelligent and so marvellously patient with the children.' Later, others were to paint less glowing descriptions of Dookie's personality. Perhaps the move to Buckingham Palace upset him: soon afterwards, Crawfie noted that he had become rather sour-natured. One day he bit the hand of Lord Lothian, who was visiting the Palace. With great fortitude his lordship insisted it was nothing. 'All the same, he bled all over the floor,' noted Princess Elizabeth.

Dogs were not the only animal companions of the York family. During the week, the peace and beauty of country life at Windsor gave way to a tall, narrow house in London. Downstairs, the Duchess had installed an aviary of Australian canaries in the garden room. On the top floor were the nurseries, comfortable, sunny rooms that opened on to a landing beneath a big glass dome, round which stood some thirty or so toy horses on wheels. In her book *The Little Princesses*, Crawfie described how each horse had its own saddle and bridle, kept in immaculate condition by their owners.

The house, right opposite a bus stop, was neither large nor splendid. On winter nights the children would watch out for the little ponies trotting home at the end of a long day drawing their costermongers'

1942 at Windsor with second generation corgi, Crackers, and Choo Choo, described by the King as 'an animated dish-cloth'.

carts. In the early 1930s there was still much horse-drawn traffic, and Lilibet and Margaret were always anxious about any horse which looked over-worked or weary. Both children were unspoiled, with unsophisticated tastes. For a time their favourite game, laid out on a wooden table, was a large farm with animals bought from Woolworths.

Ponies and riding were always part of the little Princesses' lives. By the mid-1930s Peggy, the fat little Shetland given to Elizabeth by George V, had been passed down to Margaret. The differences in the personalities of the ponies she now rode intrigued Elizabeth. The importance of getting to know and understand your pony was instilled into her by Owen, a groom who had been with the royal family for many years.

Owen taught them the rudiments of riding, but not the advanced aids from which Princess Anne was to benefit in later years. Double bridles were considered the correct tack in those days, and the little Princesses with their small fingers had to cope with a fistful of reins. Owen took enormous pride in his royal charges, and in return became Princess Elizabeth's first hero. The King made them all laugh one day when, in answer to a question about some horse-riding plan, he replied, 'Don't ask me, ask Owen. Who am I to make suggestions?'

Out of a stream of small ponies, some were a success, but others were not. It would be a mistake to think that because a horse belongs to a royal stable it is automatically a paragon of high breeding or perfectly behaved. They were not usually expensive: 45 guineas is the price recorded for one of Princess Elizabeth's ponies. George, a little pit pony, was a gift from the miners of a Durham colliery. Unfortunately, George did not adapt to his new circumstances, proving wayward and obstinate. He went to Balmoral and made friends among the Highland ponies. Next came Snowball, a small, dock-tailed Welsh cob bought in Ireland. He too could be remarkably naughty when so inclined, whirling round in circles and giving the Princess a lesson in the vagaries of horsey unpredictability. Greylight took his place: about 12 hands high, good-looking, well-mannered and the perfect child's pony.

The Duke and Duchess enjoyed fourteen years of happy family life before the Abdication changed their lives, and those of their daughters, forever. But, like children the world over, the little Princesses were excited by the move to the vast spaces of Buckingham Palace. The first thing they did on arrival was to arrange their collection of toy horses in a long row down the corridor outside their rooms. Grooming baskets and polishing cloths were neatly packed into a basket at the end. The whole toy stable was still there on Princess Elizabeth's wedding morning in 1947.

The Palace had been unoccupied during the reign of their uncle David, and its marble magnificence seemed unwelcoming. The chil-

*In wartime Britain, horses were used on the royal farm. While
Queen Elizabeth took the reins during harvest time at
Sandringham, the King and his daughters followed on bicycles.*

dren were housed in nurseries unused for many years. Curtains had a
habit of falling off their poles when drawn by a parlourmaid, and the
mice scratched all night. When The Palace vermin catcher was sent to
the nurseries to see about the problem, Princess Elizabeth looked
dubiously at the variety of traps he had produced. 'Can't we just wait
up at night and when it comes out, pop it into a bag and secretly let it
out into the garden next day?' she asked.

With Dookie and Jane installed in dog baskets in the day nursery,
the first priority for the two Princesses was to find the quickest way
into the gardens. The walk took five minutes. For them, the best part of
Palace life was the garden. Glad of a breath of fresh air after a day
spent fulfilling official functions, the Queen would often join them out
there, receiving an enthusiastic welcome from children and dogs.

With its large lake, trees and shrubs, the Palace gardens are visited
by a wide selection of birds. A population of ducks were a special
attraction. One duck had the habit of laying her eggs outside the
Palace grounds in nearby St James's Park. When they were hatched
she would march the little fluffy ducklings back to the Palace and into
the gardens, while the police stopped the traffic and opened the gates.

With the outbreak of World War II, the royal family's lives were to change radically once again. The chief landmark of each year – so far as the children were concerned – was the summer holiday at Balmoral. In the spring of 1939 the King and Queen had gone to Canada and the United States on an official visit; but, despite the storm clouds gathering, they had promised their daughters that nothing would interfere with the much-needed break at Balmoral. Not long after their arrival, the King and Queen had to hurry back to London in view of the rapidly deteriorating political situation.

When war was declared they decided it was best to leave their daughters in the safety of the Scottish Highland retreat, where they were happy with their tribe of dogs and a trusted staff to look after them. Princess Elizabeth was now proficient at driving a pony cart, and both she and Princess Margaret found many interests to explore. They discovered wildlife. At Ballater they could even see the nearly extinct ptarmigan, and they viewed roe deer, golden plovers and hawks.

All through the 'phoney war', when nobody knew how the German attack was going to be made, the royal children stayed on at Balmoral. Frosts darkened the heather, and the hares put on their coats of winter white as an early fall of snow transformed the countryside. Overnight in the unheated rooms, the Princesses' sponges and flannels, together with their drinking water, froze hard.

The Princesses, true sprigs of royal hardiness, were never daunted. Before lessons each day, they were out to attend to their ponies. In 1938 they had gone for more advanced riding lessons at Horace Smith's stables in Berkshire (his daughter later taught Princess Anne). They were given mounted exercises to improve their balance and confidence, and taught to walk, trot and canter without stirrups. They were judged competent to start jumping. But the outbreak of war had put an end to these lessons.

In mid-December the family were reunited. The King and Queen, refusing to be parted any longer from their daughters, brought them south to Windsor, where they remained throughout the war. The Princesses soon learned to climb into their siren suits when the air raid warnings went; gathering up their dogs, they would descend into the dungeons which served as shelters. Living as normal a life as possible with their dogs and ponies and some evacuees for company, they lived for Friday nights when their parents came down from London.

In this comparative isolation, dog companions became more important than ever. When the photographer Lisa Sheridan and her husband arrived to take pictures of the Princesses on a hot, sweltering day, they found Princess Margaret reading aloud to Jane the corgi from her favourite book, *The Children of the New Forest*. With Princess Mar-

The King gives a hand rounding up the pigs at Sandringham after the war.

garet lying on Queen Victoria's brocade-covered couch, Jane was stretched out in splendour as though listening to every word. Still on display at Royal Lodge is the Queen Mother's favourite picture of the era, which shows a back view of the two Princesses playing a duet on the piano. Lying beneath Princess Margaret's right foot is Jane, with a look of vacant bliss on her face. Jane's presence, the Queen told Mrs Sheridan, was an essential part of the picture's composition.

Each Christmas the Princesses staged, wrote and acted in a pantomime. Wherever they went, the sisters were accompanied by the corgis. Crackers, the ebullient son of Jane, seemed particularly anxious not to be left out. Performances were staged in the Waterloo Chamber, scene of many a royal banquet. Watched by some invited guests, a rehearsal of the grand finale was taking place when the ten-year-old Princess Margaret was seen cautiously descending the staircase dressed in a crinoline. Just as she was about to make her curtsey to the Prince – played by Princess Elizabeth – there was a sudden rustle of skirts as Crackers emerged and wriggled off stage.

The pantomimes, which certainly helped to take everyone's mind off the dark days of the war, nearly always contained a surprise element. One year, when *Cinderella* was being staged, the part of the Fairy Godmother was taken by a large white angora rabbit. The rabbit had already provided Princess Margaret with enough wool to spin a really good pair of gloves, and had been chosen for the part because of her ability to look in the right direction when someone pointed. Dressed in a bonnet and shawl, the rabbit leaped obediently round as directed.

Somewhat naturally, the corgis were intensely interested in this performance. Their high-pitched barking and their determined scratching on the door of the Waterloo Chamber had caused more than one interruption. Firmly removed by a page and shut into another room, they nevertheless escaped on several occasions. Whenever this happened, the cry of 'Fairy Godmother' went up and there was chaos for a few minutes as the dogs yapped, chairs were overturned and Princess Margaret swiftly removed the quivering Fairy Godmother to a place of safety.

Not long after the beginning of the war there was great sadness when Dookie, the favourite corgi, died. He was greatly missed by the family. This was followed by a tragedy hitting Carol, who developed fits and had to be put down, leaving Jane and Crackers as the mainstay.

Crackers had evolved into a dog of beautiful looks and charming character. 'He has the sweetest nature,' the King remarked to friends. 'The labradors must often try his patience but he is never aggressive and is always chummy and cheerful with them.' With his equable temperament and fine looks Crackers would have made an ideal father; but, as it happened, he suffered from the same misfortune that had afflicted Dookie – he was not interested in the opposite sex.

It was Rozavel Lady Jane, his mother, who ruled the roost at Windsor during most of the war years. Like so many corgis she did not show her age, even when eight years old. Princess Margaret gave her a party, so the event has been remembered. But in 1944 Jane's life was ended when she was run over and killed by one of the estate workers in Windsor Park. Princess Elizabeth at once sat down and wrote a note to the driver telling him she knew he was not to blame. There was little traffic during the war and Jane had developed a habit of running across the road – an impulse that proved fatal.

To take Jane's place, Princess Elizabeth was given a corgi puppy named Susan which lodged in her mistress's sitting room at the Castle for the remainder of the war. She later became famous when she accompanied Princess Elizabeth and the Duke of Edinburgh to Lord Mountbatten's home, Broadlands, on their honeymoon. Her official name, registered with the Kennel Club, was Hickathrift Pippa; her father was rather resplendently registered as Glamorous Knight. It was Susan who was to assure the royal corgi succession. After the war, when the royal family were staying once more at Balmoral, Susan was flown down to London in the Royal Mail plane and was mated to another of Mrs Gray's champions – Rozavel Lucky Strike. Sugar and

The King with his labrador retriever, Glen. A superlative shot, one of Bertie's chief pleasures was training his gun dogs.

Honey were in the litter. Honey went to Queen Elizabeth, by now the Queen Mother, and Sugar – distinguished by his white feet and socks – became a special pet of Prince Charles's, when years later Princess Elizabeth's first-born began to take notice of dogs.

During the war the King and Queen had a near escape when a bomb fell on Buckingham Palace, demolishing the chapel and swimming pool. Knowing what it was like to have her home bombed, the Queen toured the badly hit East End of London, comforting those who had suffered the same fate. On one of her frequent visits with the King, she noticed a woman crying. Her terrier, frightened by the bombs, had hidden beneath a pile of rubble and was refusing to move. 'Perhaps I can help,' said the Queen. 'I am rather good with dogs.' So she talked patiently to the little dog and eventually persuaded it to come out of hiding.

The Princesses were still able to enjoy riding during the war years. But with staff at Windsor cut to the minimum, and only one groom, they had to catch their own horses, groom them and put on their saddles and bridles. Princess Elizabeth had now graduated to Comet, a Welsh-Arab Cross of 13.3 hands, while Greylight had been passed down to Princess Margaret. It was a time of undreamed-of freedom. The two Princesses were trusted to ride on their own, to open and close farm gates, and often took a picnic of jam sandwiches and lemonade in a saddle bag as they cantered over the deserted acres of Windsor Great Park.

When Comet was outgrown, Jock came into Princess Elizabeth's life. Of obscure origins, with a fiery streak, Jock had been bought and used by her father as a deer pony and proved to be the most extraordinary character out of all her ponies. His colour was a unique bronze. Not exactly the conventional safe child's pony, Jock was always game for a gallop and would sometimes shy violently. All the same, Princess Elizabeth built up an enormous bond of understanding with Jock. She broke him to harness and drove him about the estate, and has gone on record as saying that 'Jock taught me more than any other horse'. He lived to a venerable age, and when he went into semi-retirement at Windsor proved extremely wily about being caught. Horses seldom forget a voice and the Queen remained the only person who could catch him without difficulty.

Although horse shows were necessarily restricted during the war, anyone who had any sort of carriage they could harness to a horse looked them out and used them in place of motor transport. In 1943 both Princesses took prizes at Windsor, driving a fell pony called Gypsy drawing a utility vehicle. This was something of a triumph. Gypsy had become much too strong for riding and was soon unsuitable for driving as well. Originally from Scotland, she was sent back to stud at Balmoral and later bred several foals of the strong fell breed in

Monaveen, the race horse shared by Princess Elizabeth and her mother, won three races for them. When he broke a leg and had to be put down in 1950, the Princess was so upset, she resolved never to own another steeplechaser.

which the Queen now takes a special interest.

While the Princesses were relatively safe with their dogs and horses at Windsor, another of the royal animals had played an active and heroic part in the war. One of the medals of which the King had been proudest had been awarded to one of his pigeons. The royal pigeons had served with distinction in both world wars, and had been specially trained to fly over water. This experience paid off splendidly when a bird named Royal Blue saved the lives of a group of airmen. Their plane, carrying Royal Blue, was returning from the Continent when it was shot down. After the forced landing, the British team released Royal Blue, who flew straight to Sandringham. A successful rescue was then carried out. Royal Blue was awarded the Dicken Medal for gallantry – the highest honour given to animals for war service.

Rehabilitation was slow after the war. A long period of grey austerity descended, and at Sandringham extensive renovations were needed. But the war had had some good effects: the partridge population, untroubled by shooting parties, had increased, and a fine stud of Suffolk Punches had been developed. These strong and magnificent animals had been used on the farm during the war; and, with the continuing petrol shortages, they were used to pull ploughs for many years afterwards.

It was left to King George VI to alter the shooting arrangements on the estate. Since then no artificial rearing has been undertaken at Sandringham, and only wild birds are shot, The King's favourite shooting companion at that time was Sandringham Glen, a yellow labrador which was a brilliant worker and devoted to his master. In fact Glen's colour was nearer cream than yellow, and with his black nose and black-rimmed eyes he was a most-distinctive-looking dog.

The years immediately following the war saw the restoration of the fortunes of the royal studs with the victory of Hypericum in the Thousand Guineas of 1946. This was followed by a line of high-class winners in the 1950s. By then both Queen Elizabeth and her elder daughter were taking a keen interest in bloodstock breeding. Horse racing had become very much of a family concern.

Bertie and Elizabeth celebrated their Silver Wedding a few years before his death in 1952. His fragile health had been strained by a job he had never wanted, and a war in which Britain had come close to disaster more than once. The King's last day was spent out shooting, wearing an electrically warmed waistcoat against the cold. In the evening he paid two visits to the Sandringham kennels to inquire after the well-being of a dog which had damaged its paw during the day's shooting. To the King it was a natural act of consideration towards the welfare of a beloved companion. The next morning, when his valet brought him an early pot of tea, he found that the King had died in his sleep.

It took the Queen Mother, as she then became, some little time to show the world the same gently smiling face to which they had become accustomed for the best part of thirty years. Apart from her work, which she has described as 'the rent you pay for your place on earth', she has wisely kept up all her main interests. Grandchildren have been the great joys of her life since the death of her husband, and she is still surrounded by dogs.

The Queen Mother's dogs go with her to Royal Lodge at weekends, and to her house on the Balmoral estate, Birkhall. They are given a never-ending supply of chocolate drops, which she says are good for them as they contain vitamins. At one time she had a corgi mother and daughter respectively named Honey and Bee. Heather, the grand-daughter, gave birth to a fifth generation. Blackie, a seventh-generation corgi, was the Queen Mother's close companion, together with Geordie, his half brother. Geordie (now deceased) is the father of Smoky, who has distinguished herself by developing outstanding retrieving abilities. The Queen sometimes uses her for picking up birds after shoots, since she is as gentle and soft-mouthed as any well-trained labrador.

The Queen Mother's affinity with all dogs, not just her own, had

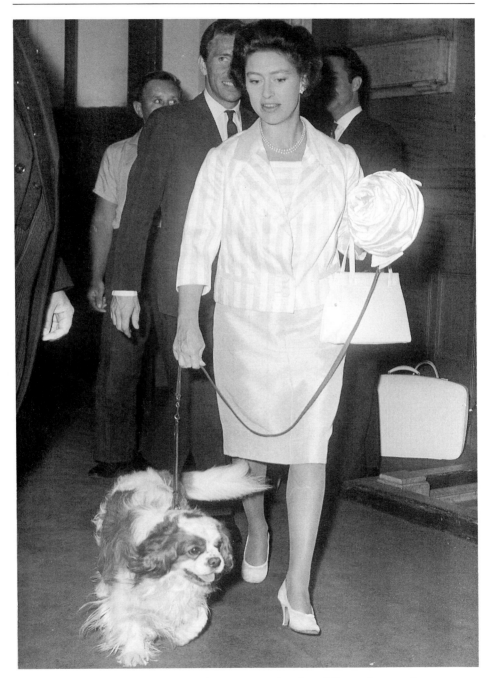

*Princess Margaret, then married to Lord Snowdon and
accompanied by a King Charles spaniel, embarks from King's Lynn
to join the Queen on a holiday.*

been graphically revealed when she coaxed a frightened terrier out of the East End rubble during the war. In the early 1950s Princess Margaret acquired a puppy of a new breed for the royal family – a sealyham called Johnny. She took it with her to Balmoral, where a week later she developed a bad case of measles. During her illness, her mother looked after Johnny, with the result that his affections remained firmly with Queen Elizabeth. Proof of Johnny's allegiance was seen in a film of Prince Charles's christening, when he dashed in and out of the room, hastily licking the new grandmother's hand on his way.

Every July the Queen Mother is in residence at Sandringham again. She loves the wind off the North Sea and the scent of salt in the air. Bracing walks along the shore are taken with the dogs, and she usually attends the Sandringham Cottage Horticultural Society show held on the last Wednesday of July. While at Sandringham she always pays a visit to the royal stables and stud, for horse-racing is her great passion.

'Why do you keep half of Mummy's mares at Sandringham and the other half at Wolferton?' Queen Elizabeth II once asked Michael Oswald, who manages the stud in both places.

'Well, if I didn't, Ma'am,' Oswald replied, 'one groom would think he hadn't had his fair share.'

'Yes,' replied the Queen, 'that's the effect Mummy seems to have on people.'

When the King died, his fourteen racehorses were inherited by his daughter, Queen Elizabeth II. From then on, the Queen Mother has concentrated on steeplechasing, while the Queen's horses only run on the Flat. Their common interest binds mother and daughter closer, and they can often be seen together at race meetings or visiting the studs with baskets of carrots.

The winter of 1961–2 brought the Queen Mother the best National Hunt season she has ever enjoyed. She had eight horses in training, of which the most outstanding were Laffy, Double Star and The Rip, and she finished the season with twenty-four successes. As a leading National Hunt racehorse owner she is thoroughly professional in her approach. At Clarence House she is on the 'Blower' – the same race course commentary as that relayed in the betting shops – and she often watches the racing on television.

The Queen Mother races under the colours of her Strathmore grandfather: blue and buff stripes worn with a black cap and gold tassel. She chooses her horses herself and has a say in where they shall run. Her knowledge is respected in the racing world, and she talks to her trainer before and after a race. Star of the paddock and toast of the Turf, she is regarded not only as a great lady but as a great sportswoman through good luck and bad.

*Princess Margaret meeting a cheetah at London Zoo, introduced by
keeper Jim Aldis, in 1967.*

6
THE QUEEN AND PRINCE PHILIP

If the Queen comes in wearing a tiara the
corgis lie on the carpet in a mood of depression.

The Queen has a string of historic houses set in rolling acres, an unrivalled collection of jewellery and is often said to be the world's richest woman. Yet one thing escapes her: the breeding of a Derby winner. Her horses have won every other British classic, so not unnaturally this is her racing ambition.

The Queen's intense interest in bloodstock breeding took root during the war, when she made frequent visits to the royal stud and came to know the history and lineage of every horse there. Watching her first Derby in 1945, when it was still run at Newmarket instead of Epsom, was the fulfilment of five years of practical study. There was a war being fought, and the royal family were determined to keep up the public's morale. The mere presence of the eager, eighteen-year-old Princess Elizabeth had the desired effect. With horse-racing in her blood she was to become, in the words of her racing manager, Lord Carnarvon, 'a complete expert in this field'. By the time she was twenty, the future Queen had acquired most of the foundation of her knowledge of bloodstock, which is now formidable.

But the Queen's love of horses is by no means restricted to the pedigree elite of the equine world. On the morning before her wedding day in 1947, the Princess stood at a Buckingham Palace window watching the beloved Windsor Greys being rehearsed for her bridal procession with the Irish State Coach. The Princess knew each horse by name, and noted that two of them, Angela and Lilian, had been chosen as outriders. But on the way back from the Abbey she saw that Angela was missing from the procession. Later that day she found time to go down to the Royal Mews and ask the Superintendent what had gone wrong. The horse, it turned out, had gone lame and had been withdrawn from the return drive to spare her discomfort. Poor Angela had to give up her place in the procession, but the incident is typical of the present Queen's concern for all the animals which come under her domain.

Perhaps the proudest animal of the wedding day was Susan, the Princess's corgi which accompanied the newly-weds as they drove down the Mall in their landau after the ceremony. Amidst all the austerity of post-war Britain, the wedding had brought a welcome blaze of pageantry to the crowds lining the streets on that grey

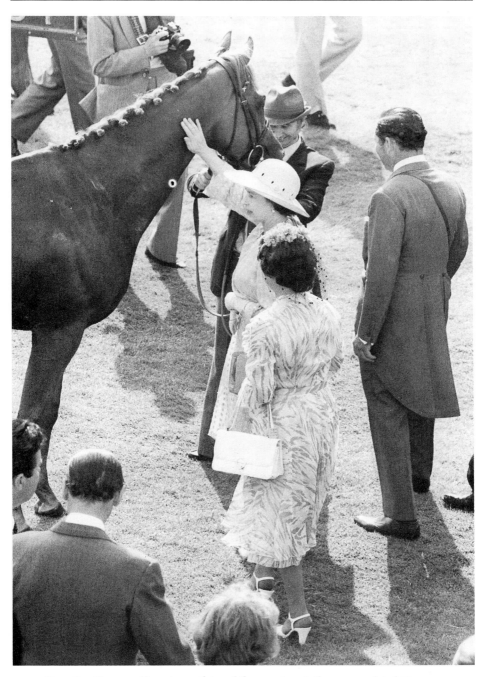

For the Queen, there's nothing like a win at the races. Lighting up when her horse, Buttress won at Ascot in 1979, the Queen still has her hopes set on the Derby.

Giant swap. The Queen and Prince Philip, together with Lord Mountbatten and former Prime Minister Edward Heath admire Chia Chia at the London Zoo. The giant panda was a gift from the Chinese in exchange for some of the almost extinct Père David's deer.

November day. Seeing Susan perched in place, ears pricked, the crowds let out an extra cheer.

The Queen's first racehorse was a wedding gift from the Aga Khan. A seven-month-old foal of impeccable breeding, Astrakhan turned out to have weak forelegs, and, after a brief though not undistinguished career which included one win, was retired to the royal paddocks at Hampton Court.

It was during the problems with Astrakhan that the present Queen Mother asked trainer Peter Cazalet to look out for a promising steeplechaser. She proposed owning it in partnership with her elder daughter, and by the spring of 1949 the eight-year-old Irish-bred gelding, Monaveen, a descendant of the 1920 Derby winner Spion Kop, was in training at Cazalet's stables in Kent. The share was a straight 'two legs each'. Racing in Princess Elizabeth's colours, Monaveen had some encouraging wins.

The King, the Queen and the two Princesses were there to watch Monaveen's first Grand National at Aintree. Princess Elizabeth's tension as she watched from the royal box was plain for all to see. But after taking the lead for the first half of the race Monaveen drew back, finishing fifth. If it came as a tremendous emotional let-down, the Princess did not let it show as she congratulated the winning owner.

There was always tomorrow. In any case the royal owners felt they had little to complain about: in one season Monaveen had brought the partners £3293 in four races.

Perhaps it was fortunate that the Princess was abroad at the end of November 1951 when Monaveen ran at Hurst Park. Queen Elizabeth, as mentor, and left with a specific request to relay every detail of the race to her daughter, was there to cheer him on as the royal hope appeared among the leaders on the second time round the course. But at the water jump he went off balance and landed with twisted legs, flinging his jockey over his neck. Tony Grantham, the jockey, was knocked out but sustained no lasting injury; Monaveen broke a leg and had to be put down. It was Queen Elizabeth's unhappy job to break the news gently on the telephone to her daughter. Just how much it upset the Princess was shown by the fact that afterwards she never owned another steeplechaser. From then on, Princess Elizabeth concentrated solely on flat racing.

In 1952, as the new Queen, overnight Elizabeth found herself in possession of her father's racehorses. She came close to winning the

The Queen with former President Reagan at Windsor during the Presidential visit of 1982. The Queen's black mare Burmese carried her faithfully on seventeen Birthday Parades, while Centennial has been ridden by Prince Charles. Both mounts came from Canada.

The Queen was amused when Geordie Bowman's carriage horses, Gruffy and J.C., 'curtseyed' at Windsor. Prince Philip often takes part in carriage driving competitions with Geordie, a scrap-merchant.

Derby in her coronation year with Aureole, home-bred in her father's stud, where she had first seen him as a week-old foal. Aureole stemmed from two generations of Derby winners; according to his pedigree he had everything – including a highly strung and excitable temperament. Even his royal owner once had to duck when offering him an apple (he only liked sweet ones) – he bucked and kicked, scattering the royal party. Aureole probably had more attention lavished on him than any horse the Queen had ever owned; eventually, she decided that he needed special treatment from a Harley Street physiotherapist, and this had a calming effect for a while. Aureole subsequently won several major races. At the 1953 Derby, everything had been done beforehand to keep the horse calm when a racegoer opened an umbrella near him as he left the paddock. The colt was disturbed and, with little time for his jockey to settle him down, made a bad start. Overtaking in spectacular fashion halfway through the race, with the Queen jumping up and down in the royal box, Aureole finished second, four lengths behind Sir Victor Sassoon's Pinza.

According to Jockey Club rules, a horse can only have one attempt at the Derby. However, Aureole conducted himself brilliantly in the next season, when the Queen became that year's winning owner. But even today, some thirty-five years later, despite other impressive successes and winnings the Queen is still not the owner or breeder of a Derby victor.

Prince Philip is President of the Shire Horse Society and enjoys driving these strong working horses with their long silky hair growing from the fetlock.

It was a shy thirteen-year-old, already steeped in a world of horses, who first met her future husband at Dartmouth Naval College where Prince Philip of Greece was a naval cadet. Philip, of Greek-Danish extraction, was to renounce his titles as Prince of Greece and Denmark in his wartime striving to obtain British nationality, and served in the Royal Navy as Lieutenant Mountbatten.

He belonged to that group of European royalty sent into exile as a result of twentieth-century wars and changes of political persuasion. Almost from the start, Prince Philip's life was one of challenge. His family escaped from Greece, their lives under threat, with their infant son hastily tucked away in a orange crate. His father had been imprisoned by revolutionaries; only the direct intervention of George V brought about his release and enabled the family to leave on a British destroyer.

Meanwhile two of Prince Andrew's brothers, King Constantine and Prince Nicholas, together with their wives, made a midnight escape in a primitive steamer bound for Palermo in Sicily. Princess Nicholas, mother of Princess Marina who later became the Duchess of Kent, was the daughter of the former Grand Duchess Helen of Russia. In their headlong flight she had left behind a hoard of precious jewellery and other valuables inherited from Russia. When some of the turmoil had died down, a fourth brother, Prince Christopher, bravely volunteered to rescue them.

Princess Nicholas gave her brother-in-law strict instructions. He was to bring back with him two suitcases filled with money and securities, a wooden box containing the jewellery, and last, but definitely not least, her elderly Persian cat, called Pussy. Prince Christopher made good the first part of his mission undetected. Weighed down with bursting suitcases and an overflowing jewel box which threatened to shed assorted rings and tiaras along the quay, Prince Christopher had just swung the cat basket into a dinghy when the outraged Pussy let out a loud and protesting wail. Conscious of the unwelcome attention drawn to the departing entourage, the Prince rowed like one possessed. Having elbowed himself and his impedimenta on to a boat bound for Brindisi, he arrived safe at last on Italian territory.

The voyage to freedom was largely spent in trying to pacify the uprooted Pussy. But his troubles were not over even then. They had to spend the night at a hotel, where the cat ran wildly down the corridors, taking refuge under strange beds. All that remained was a train journey to Palermo, where this troublesome cargo could be reunited with its owner. Mindful of his sister-in-law's instructions both to guard the jewels and to allow Pussy as much exercise as possible, the prince found a lead, and with the jewel case under his arm walked the cat up and down the platform whenever the train stopped. Trains, however, were even less to Pussy's taste than boats. Having escaped from the carriage, she was found covered in black soot and was still black when finally handed over to her anxious mistress at Palermo. 'What have you done to the poor thing?' she demanded of her exhausted brother-in-law.

'What,' he cried, 'has she not done to me!'

After their escape from Greece Prince Philip's family took refuge at Kensington Palace, and from there they moved to Paris. Philip found some outlet for his active disposition when he stayed with his aunt Sophie, formerly Queen of Greece. He rode his first pony at the age of four, hanging on to its mane as it trotted eagerly along the sandy shores of the Baltic. By the age of six he had learned to control a pony. At seven he was racing with his cousin, King Michael of Romania, as they galloped along the Black Sea coast near Constanza. Unlike Elizabeth, his future wife, Philip had no formal riding instruction during his early years. This do-it-yourself attitude may well have had something to do with his later skill at polo. He was once described as 'not a stylist, but fast and tough', and the secret of his expertise lay in an intelligently organized and flexible approach mixed with a very necessary dash of aggression. A more thorough training came later, when the Prince was sent to school at Gordonstoun. Here the boys not only received riding instruction, but were taught stable management and were expected to look after the ponies.

Riding down the Mall for the Trooping the Colour ceremony in 1972, the Queen and the Duke of Edinburgh wear black armbands in remembrance of the recent death of her uncle, the Duke of Windsor.

Although horses were never the Prince's consuming passion as a boy, both he and the Queen are alike in that they gained their horse sense from experience. The Queen and Prince Philip will talk about a horse in terms of character, something that cannot be learned from books.

The horse-loving Queen rides regularly throughout the year. Sometimes, if the weather is bad or she has little time, she will use the covered riding schools at Buckingham Palace and Windsor. It was in the indoor riding school at the Palace that she used to practise her side-saddle riding for the annual Trooping the Colour.

The biggest collection of royal horses is at the Royal Mews at Windsor, where the riding horses used by the royal family are stabled in loose boxes. A separate yard is kept for the polo ponies which compete at Smith's Lawn, Windsor during the polo season; yet another section is reserved for the carriage horses. The Windsor Greys and Cleveland Bays, used for ceremonial duties in London, often have a few weeks off at Windsor. All have their own harness and tack rooms where saddles, bridles and carriage driving equipment is kept. There is a strict rule that immediately after use all tack must be meticulously cleaned, which is done by a team of grooms and stable girls.

Now whole-hearted supporters of the Worldwide Fund for Nature, the royal family would sooner forget this picture showing an 8ft 9in tiger shot by Prince Philip in Nepal in 1961.

For many years the Queen's favourite riding horse was a beautiful black-brown mare of 15.3 hands by the name of Betsy. Always well-mannered and a good ride, but with no pretensions to high pedigree, Betsy had been bought from a local farmer. With the Queen on Betsy and Prince Philip on Mele-Kush, a horse of the Akhal-Teke breed given to him by the former Soviet President Mr Khrushchev, the royal family spent some of their happiest hours together riding in the Home Park at Windsor, with the young Prince Charles on Greensleeves and Princess Anne on William.

Sanction, a brown gelding foaled in 1978, is probably now the Queen's favourite ride. His sire was the thoroughbred polo pony Sanbal, and his dam an Argentine mare called Carnarita. A full brother to three of Prince Charles's polo ponies, Sanction combines a responsive temperament with reliability. Greenshield is a bay gelding, born at Sandringham in 1970; the Queen rides him but Prince Charles has also used him on the polo field. Centennial, a black, 17 hands Canadian police horse of the same age, is sometimes ridden by Prince Philip and is also used by Prince Charles as a parade charger; he has an impeccable temperament. Reneau, a chestnut gelding foaled in 1973, is an Arab-Barb from Algeria, originally a present from the

*Wild animals, however cuddly, are no respecters of royalty and the
Queen wore gloves to handle this koala bear when visiting Australia
in 1970.*

President of Algeria to Prince Philip, and now ridden by Prince
Edward.

The Queen likes to have a comfortable ride – which is not to say that
she wants a dull, routine horse. When she is at Windsor, the Royal
Mews is geared up to produce a selection of suitable horses at any time
they are required. It can take up to 150 horses at a time, but there is
constant movement of animals from one royal residence to another. It
is a rare event when one or other of the Queen's horses is not travelling
in her olive-green, white-lined horseboxes.

The Stud Groom at Windsor usually receives his orders for the next
day from a page on the previous evening. Unless the Queen asks for a
specific horse, he will make his selection from the mounts which are in
prime condition and available at the time. The Stud Groom will nearly
always go with the Queen, riding at a reasonable distance behind or
going ahead to unlock the park gates with one of the keys which he
always carries.

A sense of confidence and comradeship with the horse is important
to the Queen, and she rides with elastic-sided safety stirrups and a
sheepskin fitted over the saddle. Jumping is something she nowadays
leaves to Princess Anne and Prince Charles, but the type of exercise –

flat-out gallop or gentle trot – is chosen to suit the mood, temperament and condition of the horse she is riding. If she is taking any of her dogs there will be stops for them to catch up.

Perhaps the most famous of the Queen's parade horses has been Burmese. A gift from the Royal Canadian Mounted Police, the faithful black mare carried the Queen at the ceremony of Trooping the Colour for eighteen years. In 1986, the year of the Queen's sixtieth birthday, she attended her last Trooping the Colour on horseback; and the following year Burmese was officially retired. So in 1987 the Queen drove to Horse Guards Parade, where the Trooping the Colour takes place, in a phaeton built for Queen Victoria in 1842. Burmese, however, was still there in her more usual role of police horse. As the Queen drove past her on her way to the Parade, the twenty-six-year-old favourite pricked her ears in joyful recognition.

It was Burmese which had kept her composure on the alarming occasion in 1981 when a young man broke from the crowds watching the ceremony and fired a gun – containing blanks – at the Queen. Immediately, Prince Philip, escorting her on a mount a few feet behind, rushed ahead to provide protection, as did Prince Charles. The Queen had to demonstrate her fine horsemanship to control Burmese, which had been with her on many a Trooping the Colour but had never had occasion to hear shots. The Queen not only brought Burmese under control; she even managed to look round to reassure herself that neither her husband nor their eldest son had been shot.

Even when on holiday at Balmoral, the estate in the Scottish Highlands where the royal family stay between mid-August and mid-October, the hard-working Queen always puts in several hours of work a day on her official 'boxes'. Once the corgis are settled, however, and she has put on the comfortable country clothes kept from year to year at the castle, she relaxes into the rural, sporting atmosphere of the place.

The horses will have arrived before the royal family. They travel in horseboxes, by train, or in trailers pulled by Land Rover. They are in frisky condition after their long journey, and the Queen visits them in their stables soon after she arrives. Prince Philip, who takes a keen interest in the cattle on the estate, sends for a report on the Balmoral farm. Then there are the gun dogs – mostly labradors – some of whom will have grown from puppyhood since the previous year. They are kept in separate kennels and will be joined by the gun dogs owned by the royal children as well as guests' dogs. It is during the two-month late summer break that the Queen walks and rides and devotes regular time to the training of the labrador puppies, one of her main Balmoral hobbies.

Prince Philip assumes general responsibility for the estate;

The Queen with her winning filly, Carrozza, ridden by Lester Piggot in 1957.

although the Queen is overall landlord of royal property, he will take decisions such as whether to retain the Ayrshire milking herds or to dispense with the 'Blondes of Balmoral' (a breed of beef cattle) without consulting 'the landlord', busy as she is – even on holiday – with state affairs. Some agricultural interests have turned out better than others. Some of the cattle, including several bulls bred at Balmoral, have won numerous prizes. But a flock of Soay sheep of prehistoric descent whose adventures would almost fill a book, proved difficult to round up, even with dogs, and eventually had to be kept under cover during the winter and fed.

At Balmoral there are some 400 acres of arable land, mainly used for growing winter feed for the horses and livestock. As well as the cattle and sheep, about fourteen stalking ponies are kept. The estate holds over two thousand red deer, as well as a grouse moor of some 6000 acres, and some rare ptarmigan on the high peaks.

Game is one of the great attractions here. In recent years, though, the grouse on the moors surrounding the castle have suffered from a disease, a conundrum which Prince Philip is trying to solve. With the grouse population in decline, shooting has been restricted.

Prince Philip has also taken a particular interest in the problem of maintaining natural wintering grounds for the red deer, whose grazing habits have prevented natural regeneration of the trees. He has fenced off some 50 acres where Caledonian pine, birch and rowan can be regrown, and opened up about 230 acres of Ballochbuie Forest where the deer can roam in their ancestral grounds.

In order to maintain a healthy stock, around 150 stags and 250 hinds are culled annually. Although picturesque to look at, the red deer are susceptible to disease; and in his speeches and writings Prince Philip has often described the necessity for selective culling. All the deer in the area are counted every February, winter deaths recorded, and a culling policy is agreed before the stalking season begins. At Balmoral, the technique used for deer is stalking – which means the animals are shot humanely – not hunting. Only the poorest beasts are shot.

On stalking expeditions, the royal party travel the rough and craggy terrain mounted on the sure-footed Highland and fell ponies. Light-coloured Haflingers, bred from a pair given by the President of Austria in 1969, are strong and versatile, and are used for riding in addition to bringing deer carcasses down from high ground. The fell ponies have a busy life. They spend six months of the year at Balmoral, where they can be hired (as can the other ponies) by the public for trekking expeditions from mid-April to the end of July. They also go to Windsor and Sandringham where a team, driven four-in-hand by Prince Philip, take part in various carriage-driving events.

Few identify themselves with the rural way of life as whole-heartedly as the British royal family. All country people at heart, they enjoy Balmoral – with its unspoilt acres – as their great annual refresher course.

The selective culling of deer and active forestry which are practised at Balmoral are both attempts to help nature achieve the right balance. Prince Philip's involvement with conservation has achieved particular success at Sandringham, where he originated a plan to save 30 acres of reclaimed saltmarsh as a wildlife sanctuary. The nearby

A keen and hard riding polo player, Prince Philip at Cowdray Park in 1953. A few years ago, arthritis in his wrists caused him to take to carriage driving instead, but the polo tradition is carried on by Prince Charles

shores of the Wash attract large numbers of duck and wildfowl, and in a rebuilt shepherd's hut at the reserve Prince Philip has spent many hours at a viewing window which gives him a panoramic view of the saltmarsh. The Prince is also the Ranger of Windsor Great Park, where he has restored about 700 acres into a well-stocked deer park which provides a beautiful background to the historic castle.

In keeping with his broad outlook, Prince Philip's devotion to animals and conservation is demonstrated also on a more wide-ranging scale as president of the World Wide Fund for Nature. His interest in ecology dates back many years; today there is widespread concern for the environment, but Prince Philip came out for this cause in 1962. As long ago as the 1950s he waged war against the use of the poisonous chemicals that were then being introduced into farming, warning that were hazardous to wildlife. Today his eldest son shares these feelings and is also passionately involved in the conservation movement.

One of the first to draw attention to the dwindling giant panda population, Prince Philip made a special trip to the Fengtongzhai Reserve in China in 1986 where he saw the new cub born to Li-Li. As one of the few privileged Westerners to see the new progeny, then only three months old and still unsexed, he was invited by one of his Chinese hosts to name it. As it was a particularly beautiful day, Prince Philip glanced at the sky and decided on Lam Tian, Chinese for 'blue sky'. Prince Philip's presence at the reserve drew attention to the need for the right sort of habitats for pandas; here they live peaceably in the company of golden monkeys, white-lipped deer and some three hundred species of rare birds.

Prince Philip is a lover of the healthy outdoor life, and his sporting interests are many and varied. Considered to be one of the best shots in the country, the Prince, accompanied by his gun dog Glenn, greatly enjoys the New Year pheasant shoot at Sandringham. As well as a plentiful supply of pheasants, the farms also have partridges and woodcock. Another, perhaps more unexpected, string to Prince Philip's bow has been greyhound racing; in 1968, his dog Camira Flash won the Greyhound Derby. The Queen and her husband continue to enjoy successes with the royal racing pigeons, a sport initiated by her great-grandfather Edward VII. She is patron of a number of pigeon racing societies and makes regular visits to the lofts where they are kept. In 1988 a racing pigeon similar in breed to the Queen's, was sold in Belgium for the equivalent of £70,000.

The sport with which Prince Philip was for many years most closely associated in the public mind was polo. Perhaps the most significant influence on Prince Philip's relationship with horses was his uncle, Lord Mountbatten. A lifelong polo enthusiast, he wrote a definitive textbook on the subject – *An Introduction to Polo* by 'Marco' – and encouraged both Prince Philip and Prince Charles to take up the game.

After the Queen's accession in 1952 Prince Philip took part in what he has described as some 'wonderful seasons, playing at Cowdray, and even more important, on Cowdray ponies'. Lord Cowdray had revived the sport on his estate in Sussex after the war, and a little later Prince Philip was the driving force behind the formation of the Household Brigade Polo Club at Smith's Lawn, Windsor, in 1956. The fast and furious game was played with enormous skill and courage by Prince Philip, as often as his commitments would allow, through the 1950s and 1960s. His enthusiasm led him to become one of the eight best players in Britain, with a handicap of five.

The Queen's knowledge of horse-breeding gives her a highly professional interest in polo. Not only does she understand the intricacies of the game, but many of the polo ponies on which Prince Philip competed, and which Prince Charles now rides, have been a result of the Queen's breeding policies. It was on Doublet, home-bred by the Queen out of a royal polo pony, that Princess Anne won the 1971 Three Day Event at Burghley.

Dressed in headscarf and comfortable country tweeds, the Queen certainly enjoys being a spectator at horse shows. On one occasion her long experience of dealing with horses was used to the benefit of other

Princess Elizabeth riding in the grounds of Royal Lodge, Windsor
shortly before her fourteenth birthday

members of the crowd. Aware that two horses had bolted and were a
menace to spectators, she advanced, caught their bridles and stopped
them, then returned them to their grooms.

With his usual dry humour, Prince Philip once described the horse
as 'the great leveller'. And polo, quite one of the most demanding
sports ever invented, had caused him many a crashing fall. 'I reckoned
fifty was quite old enough for that game,' he remarked in 1970 when
arthritis in his wrists made him decide it was time to look for another
sport.

Prince Philip took up the challenge of carriage-driving with his
usual enthusiasm and application, and trained himself at Sandringham with the help of Major Tommy Thompson, former Riding Master
of the Household Cavalry. May 1972 marked his appearance at the
Royal Windsor Horse Show with a carriage and pair. Since practising
with the Cleveland Bays from the Royal Mews whose main role is
ceremonial functions, he has succeeded as an excellent four-in-hand
driver, surmounting countryside courses set with obstacles which can
easily upset carriage and occupants. As well as putting the sport on the
map, he has competed in a number of countries and won various team
prizes, including a bronze medal at the European Championships in
Switzerland in 1981. The following year he published an excellent
book on the subject, entitled *Competition Carriage Driving*.

The Queen, too, is an excellent whip, and when they were small she enjoyed driving her younger children, Andrew and Edward, around Windsor. Although she admires excellence in all sports and likes a winner, one feature that interests her about Prince Philip's carriage-driving – of which she is a keen spectator – is that, despite the rather grand-looking equipages, a democratic spirit is very much part of things. One of Prince Philip's fellow-enthusiasts is a scrap merchant who delights in teaching his horses a few party tricks – something which would certainly be frowned upon in show-jumping or hunting circles.

At Sandringham a few years ago, George (known as 'Geordie') Bowman pulled off one of these tricks by training his horses to curtsey to the Queen when she inspected his team after a driving competition. She had seen them bend their knees before in an imitation curtsey during a competition at Windsor, but now she took the trouble to stop and tell Geordie, 'They are getting better at it!' George Bowman has ridden several times with Prince Philip in world championship events and has helped Britain win gold medals. Keeping company with royalty is not something which embarrasses him. 'Prince Philip knows I'm a scrap merchant,' he said. 'It makes no difference. Backgrounds don't come into our sport.'

The royal interest in horses often serves a purpose at semi-formal functions, when it becomes a device for putting people at their ease. Guests are told the lineage of a recent addition to the royal stables and invited to think of a witty name for the new foal. The Palace corgis, too, are known as ice-breakers – the patter of tiny paws at a private lunch party will often loosen the tongue of the most inhibited guest. But the staff are given instructions to ask visitors discreetly to refrain from offering tit-bits, which might well be unsuitable, and from handling or stroking the animals.

The Queen is now one of the most experienced British breeders of Pembrokeshire corgis, and some of her present pets are ninth-generation descendants of Susan, the little dog she was given as an eighteenth birthday present in 1944. She always chooses the sire herself, aiming for good-looking puppies that maintain the reddish colour of the original Pembrokes.

Through the ages, corgis have been brave and efficient little cattle dogs, guarding herds single-handed and rounding them up, with their teeth snapping at the beasts' heels. Breed out their tendency to snap at heels, and you breed out other corgi characteristics. The other side of the coin is that corgis are wonderful companions for children – why else would the Queen have stuck to them so faithfully? – highly intelligent, gifted at games like hide-and-seek, and affectionate towards their owners. Unfortunately, corgis do not always react well to

Above, *The little Princesses, guarded as ever by a watchful corgi after moving to Buckingham Palace when their father became King.*

Left, *The Queen has bred ten generations of corgis from Susan who lived to the grand old age of fifteen, the human equivalent of one hundred.*

uniforms, as Guardsmen on duty and policemen in the lodge at Buckingham Palace have discovered. The stamping of feet in a smart salute does something to a corgi, and they are usually kept in the background on ceremonial occcasions.

After the Queen herself, the person closest to the corgis is her childhood nursemaid, Bobo Macdonald. Miss Macdonald knows that corgis react strongly to signals. She has noted that if the Queen enters a room wearing a tiara the corgis will lie mutely on the carpet in an apparent mood of Celtic depression, but when their mistress comes through the door wearing a headscarf they are immediately animated and start jumping up and down. This is the signal for a walk, and no one knows better than the Queen's devoted maid and dresser that no matter what you say to them you cannot fool a corgi.

The Queen also has a unique breed in the shape of a dorgi – a cross between the Pembrokeshire bitches and Princess Margaret's long-haired dachshund Pipkin. The result of a chance romance, current dorgi pets are Piper, who is long-haired and Chipper, who is smooth-coated. These are the only males among the Queen's dogs; the decision to give away the male puppies in litters was taken after a fight when one of the corgis finished up with a badly injured foot.

Normally all the dogs get on well and travel together by car, train and plane between Buckingham Palace, Windsor, Sandringham and Balmoral. The only thing they dislike is the open steps leading down from aircraft, and occasionally one of them has to be carried. Staff accustomed to this problem have tried covering the back of the steps with a sheet, but corgis prefer terra firma and the royal pets have not been hoodwinked by this idea.

As children, the Queen and Princess Margaret were well aware that corgis enjoy life – with a zest that is good to see – only when fully occupied. Too many dogs potter through life with little to amuse them between one mealtime and the next, but this does not suit corgis. Among the many amusements provided for the pre-war corgis by the little Princesses were interminable games of hide-and-seek and the even greater sport of jumping over either of the mistresses whenever the opportunity occurred. Since all the Queen's children are now grown-up the corgis no longer have the stimulus of equally excitable and energetic playmates, and they often seem bored. A bored corgi is a problem corgi, which may be why the Queen has recently been reported as consulting a 'dog psychologist' who can recommend some form of occupational therapy.

The royal corgis are never sold. Some puppies, such as the males, are given away to good homes, although family sources now seem to have dried up. Prince Charles and Prince Andrew are not enamoured of the breed, and only Princess Anne has taken a Palace-bred corgi in recent years. The royal corgis are registered under the kennel name of

*The royal laugh at its heartiest was for the antics of a sheepdog
when the Queen watched some trials in Australia in 1988.*

Windsor. Windsor Loyal Subject, bred by the Queen, went to the original royal breeder, Mrs Thelma Gray, who now lives in Australia. This dog did well in Australia, winning several championships, and is much in demand as a sire.

Nor do royal corgis ever go into boarding kennels. All the same, there are times when they must part. When the Queen is away on a royal tour, the dogs are looked after by the wife of a Windsor Great Park official. She treats them as her own and sticks to the diet worked out by the Queen, which includes vitamin pills. The dogs seem to enjoy their stay in more informal surroundings. Once, one of the corgis gave birth to a litter of puppies while the Queen was away, so numbers were doubled overnight.

When she is in residence the Queen takes them for walks in the Palace grounds, dries them when wet with a special towel, and mixes their feed herself from ingredients brought in on a tray by a footman. Shadow, Myth, Fable, Smoky, Spark, Diamond and Kelpie, the ninth-generation corgis, continue to be the most cherished of all the Queen's well-loved animals.

7

THE PRINCE AND PRINCESS
OF WALES

'I'd rather be riding the horses than looking at them.'

For the Prince who has earned the unofficial title of Action Man, playing polo hard in the summer months and hunting enthusiastically in the winter has become his main form of relaxation. Horses are a way of life for this Prince. But there is also a quieter, more solitary side to his nature, and he is just as keen on fishing, shooting and bird-watching. When it was once commented on that he went fishing on Sundays, he remarked: 'I can pray when I'm fishing, but I can't fish in church.'

In his infancy and early school years Prince Charles enjoyed the affection of a variety of animals. He had his own corgi, a hamster called Chi Chi and a rabbit named Harvey. His grandmother added to this collection by giving him two South American love birds called David and Annie.

At the age of four he was put on an ancient Shetland pony called Fum, and was later taught by the same redoubtable Sybil Smith who had instructed the Queen. At first he showed little of the passion for jumping which distinguished Princess Anne. After riding at Windsor on a Welsh pony called William, his next pony, Bandit, proved something of a handful. 'He used to stand up on his hind legs and all that sort of thing,' said Prince Charles, describing his earlier experiences. 'Not being nearly as brave as my sister, which often happens, I rather got put off.'

Later, when he went away to boarding school, he was separated from the continuous pleasure given him by the companionship of his smaller pets. A working labrador's life is comparatively short, for instance – often little more than seven years. Favourite dogs had passed on when he returned home.

In 1971 he entered the Royal Naval College at Dartmouth and embarked on a decade of trial by danger, becoming the first heir to the throne to descend to earth by parachute and to win a jet pilot's licence. Not satisfied without a challenge in his life, he turned to the excitements of cross-country riding and team steeplechasing, and then to hunting.

Occasionally, however, the active Prince has to take a back seat and watch others experiencing the thrills and the tumbles. In 1981, about a month before his wedding to Lady Diana Spencer, the couple were at

Above, *Prince Charles loves playing with dogs. On this occasion Murphy, a Jack Russell puppy, became so excited he bit the heir to the throne.*

Left, *More fun with Tigger, the Prince's three-year-old Jack Russell, shown here as a puppy. Tigger has since had puppies of her own and was originally given to the Prince in 1986 by his gardening friend, Lady Salisbury.*

Ascot – he in top hat and morning coat, she in filmy dress and flower-trimmed hat. Walking towards the paddock where the horses were parading for the next race, they turned towards a side gate intending to leave the course quietly. On the way, Diana was greeted by a friend. As they remained talking, her fiancé looked pointedly at his watch: time was clearly of the essence. The discreet escape had been planned so that Charles could go and play polo at Windsor Great Park. An afternoon of being seated in the Royal Box was not to his taste, and he was later to say about race meetings, 'I'd rather be riding the horses than looking at them.'

Born into a family noted for preferring a country life atmosphere of horses and dogs, Diana had been seated on a pony at an early age. However, childhood falls did not endear her to horses. The first home she remembers was Park House on the Sandringham estate, a ten-bedroomed Victorian mansion built by Edward VII to accommodate the overflow of guests from Sandringham House. It was here, in 1961, that Diana Frances Spencer was born. The house had come into the family through Diana's mother, whose father had rented it from George V. Diana's father was at the time an equerry to the Queen.

Although there seemed scarcely a time when Charles and Diana didn't know each other, the most he would have seen of his future bride at Sandringham was the glimpse of a small girl playing energetic games with his brothers, Andrew and Edward. Both houses contained many animals. At Park House, Diana made pets of the smaller varieties: rabbits, hamsters and guinea pigs. Then there were the horses and ponies, her father's gun dog Bray, a springer spaniel called Jill and a cat known as Marmalade.

For the whole family, riding was a normal part of country life. But when she was eight, Diana suffered the first of her falls from ponies and broke an arm. Two years later, her pony Romany caught a hoof in a rabbit hole and Diana came off again. This time it took much longer to persuade her back into the saddle.

There were underlying reasons for her anxiety, for her mother had left the family and round about that time her parents got divorced. It was decided that Diana needed the stability of boarding school. In 1970, accompanied by her pet guinea pig Peanuts, she joined her sister Sarah at Riddlesworth Hall, not too far from Sandringham.

Writing about their most famous old girl in the school magazine of 1981, the headmistress recalled some distinctive aspects of Diana's personality, including 'her kindness to smaller members of the community and her love of animals as well as her considerable excellence in swimming and prowess in physical activities'. Diana won the Pets' Corner Cup and several sports prizes, though she was not an academic achiever at any of the schools she went to.

Above, *To prove she is undaunted by reptiles, the Princess of Wales lays cautious fingers on a freshwater crocodile in Darwin, Australia.*

Left, *Prince Harry on Smokey, the Shetland pony which Prince William started riding and which used to belong to Princess Anne's children.*

After finishing-school in Switzerland she was working at a small London nursery school when her sister Jane, who had married a Private Secretary to the Queen, asked her up to Balmoral to help with her new baby. There she met Prince Charles again, and, together with friends, they would picnic at Craigowan, a rather primitive fishing lodge near the River Dee in which Charles – but not Diana – would stand patiently for hours on end, casting for salmon.

Charles's name had been linked with many eligible young women, including Diana's other sister, Sarah, but a relationship between the two of them began to blossom in the late autumn of that year. Standing in a turnip field, Charles with shotgun on shoulder and Diana with cartridge bag in hand, their formal engagement became a reality.

After their dazzling wedding, Charles and Diana went to live at Highgrove in Gloucestershire, a Georgian house which Charles had fallen in love with and bought in 1980. The nine-bedroomed house with its walled garden and high cedar tree was only eight miles away from Princess Anne at Gatcombe Park, near where Charles had begun hunting with the Beaufort. The Berkeley and the Bicester, two other famous hunts, are also within reasonable distance.

Charles had come late to hunting, and Princess Anne had had to give her brother some jumping lessons in the indoor riding school at Windsor before his first day out with the Beaufort. At Gatcombe they jumped fences, with the Princess giving Charles a lead. His sister also advised him on his choice of hunters. Charles has been known to inquire at various hunts for a reasonably priced hunter; and, in the early days, his horses were not always of the best. Next he went to Leicestershire, where he now keeps two hunters, and went out with the Cottesmore, the Quorn and the Belvoir – all famous Shire hunts which can be terrifying for a beginner. Charles described one of his first experiences in a foreword to Ulrica Murray Smith's book *Magic of the Quorn*: 'When you first visit the Quorn you can't help feeling while being trampled in the rush that the majority of the field are still in training for one of Wellington's campaigns!'

Since then Charles has hunted with about fifty different packs of hounds from the four hundred in Britain. He goes out in all weathers; and, like other participants, has inevitably 'tasted the turf' on occasions, suffering some crashing falls. Prince Charles asks for no special considerations. He is much aware that the horse is the great leveller and has set safety standards by wearing a hunting cap, which he secures with a flesh-coloured chin-strap. In the blue Windsor coat with red cuffs and red facings, he arrives quietly out of the morning mists, joining the hunt with as little fuss as possible after the others have moved off.

All the hunts that Prince Charles joins conform to the Master of

Above, *The Prince and Princess of Wales in Saudi Arabia inspecting a trained hawk. Falconry is an expensive sport. Some hawks are sold for the price of a racehorse.*

Left, *Never entirely at home on horseback, the Princess of Wales joins a family ride at Sandringham, her first since she fell and broke an arm as a child.*

Confidently riding out on his Welsh Mountain pony, Topaz, Prince William gets some instruction from his aunt, the Princess Royal.

Foxhounds Association's rules. These cover the humane dispatch of the fox, and see to it that the hunt is conducted properly. In this respect, standards are now much higher than they were in the days of his ancestors.

Charles applies similar standards to fishing and shooting. He has expressed concern about some of the large-scale shoots at which reared pheasants are let loose and subjected to wholesale slaughter, sometimes accompanied by unnecessary wounding. At one time it was rumoured that Prince Charles had abandoned shooting, because he had given a pair of his Purdey shotguns to Prince Andrew. But he now shoots with family friends at Sandringham, where birds are disposed of quickly and cleanly.

Today, the anti-hunting lobby is an audible voice in the land. It has not stopped Prince Charles from hunting, a sport that virtually all royal princes and kings have enjoyed; but, as Michael Clayton, editor of *Horse and Hound*, has put it:

> He is sensitive to the arguments against hunting, but cares passionately about the conservation of wildlife and its environment, believing firmly that hunting plays a valuable role in this. Even those who are the most ardent critics of foxhunting should be aware that Prince Charles's involvement has already been a power for good in maintaining standards.

Prince Charles knows that anything he says in favour of a sport – which, after all is a blood sport – will be taken as an excuse, or a justification. But he points to the fact that without it farmers would cease to maintain the traditional landscape of the English countryside with its woodlands, coverts and hedges. Many formerly beautiful parts of the country where hunting no longer takes place have already become featureless prairies of EEC cash crops controlled by pesticides, in which hedgerows and trees, together with the wildlife that flourishes in them, are fast disappearing.

Contrary to rumour, the Princess enjoys watching polo – even when her husband loses. On this occasion at the Guard's Club, Smiths Lawn, Windsor she presented him with the runner's up medal.

*Prince Charles relaxing with a book at Balmoral accompanied by
his old companion, Harvey the labrador.*

As with his father, this approach to the balance of nature and the maintaining of natural habitats has led to a strong interest in conservation and ecology. In 1988 he became President of the College of Estate Management. Prince Charles's concern for developing farming methods that will permit conservation, and simultaneously give farmers a fair return on their investments, were among his reasons for accepting this presidency. In the same year he presented a BBC television documentary entitled *A Vision of Britain*. He was filmed taking a trip down the Thames. Both as a fisherman and as a conservationist, he was very interested in the fact that, with a reduction of pollution, the Thames has begun to support salmon again.

His interest in conservation and ecological management is, like Prince Philip's, international, and he is quick to acknowledge his father's important contribution. During a recent visit to the USA he attended two benefits in aid of Friends of Conservation. To a packed and enthusiastic audience he said:

> It has occurred to me that my father has done more for conservation than almost anyone else. He started twenty-five years ago, but now many others have become concerned. . . . We are beginning to realize the kinds of problems we have created with insecticides, industrial waste, and the commercial slaughter of animals. . . . Rainforests are the lungs of the world, important for us who live in developed countries; and without them, there won't be a habitable globe for people or animals.

On his many travels abroad Prince Charles has come across some of the more exotic animals in which he maintains an interest. He may dislike Princess Michael of Kent's Siamese cats invading his kitchen at Kensington Palace, but he cares a lot about the fate of big cats in the wild. In India and Pakistan rapidly expanding populations have impinged heavily on the regions where tigers live and breed. He is well aware, too, that in central Africa the territory of the mountain gorilla is diminishing yearly as native populations push into it to open up farms. His friendship with Laurens van der Post, the South African explorer and writer who is godfather to Prince William, has enlarged Prince Charles's understanding of these problems.

To help animals of specific areas, he has offered the weight of his name and presence to schemes aimed at saving their natural habitats. One such scheme, advanced in the late 1980s, was an approach to save the Korup rainforest of Cameroon and Nigeria. Hunters with modern weapons were decimating the jungle wildlife for their own use and profit, selling the meat and hides. The whole balance of the rainforest was under threat: leopards, chimpanzees, elephants and forest buffaloes were only a few of the species threatened. The jungle, sixty million years old, shelters a quarter of Africa's primate species, as well as four

A moment of triumph in 1980 for Prince Charles when he finished second on his steeplechaser Allibar. A few months later Allibar tragically collapsed after being exercised by the Prince. Diana wept as the gallant horse died. Shortly afterwards Charles gave up jockeying.

Prince Charles has not been called Action Man for nothing.
Hunting in the winter and playing polo in the summmer, here the
Prince rides for the Golden Eagles team in Deauville.

hundred species of trees and a whole range of birds, plants and insects. Prince Charles wanted to help the local people learn how to use farming methods that do not destroy plant and animal life.

By the time Charles had come to know and love nineteen-year-old Diana, he had a particular affection for his racehorse, Allibar. The pain as well as the pleasure of owning animals is something with which many sensitive people find it hard to come to terms. Diana was fully involved in what Prince Charles has described as 'the awful, awful tragedy of Allibar'.

Just before their marriage in 1981, Prince Charles had been competing in National Hunt racing. He had been taking huge jumps in his stride, and was keen to find the right horse to take part in the Grand Military Gold Cup, held annually at Sandown Park. His friend and trainer, Nick Gaselee, had found in Ireland a ten-year-old prize-winning gelding called Allibar, and Prince Charles formed an excellent relationship with the horse. Wearing his racing colours of scarlet with royal blue sleeves and black cap for the first time, Charles had the thrill of riding his own horse at Ludlow. In a most exciting race he came second, and returned in a glow of pleasure.

A few months later Diana was watching Prince Charles exercise Allibar at Lambourn on the Berkshire Downs, when suddenly it appeared that all was not going well. Charles began to walk Allibar back to Gaselee's yard, when the horse stumbled. Charles swiftly dismounted as Allibar sank to his knees and died. The Prince knelt by him, with Diana weeping nearby.

A veterinary surgeon later found that Allibar had suffered a massive heart attack. Although horses are prone to heart trouble, there had been no earlier suggestion of it in Allibar's case. At the age of eleven, he seemed in his prime as a steeplechaser. Both Charles and Diana were heartbroken.

With the royal wedding only a few months ahead and a heavy load of commitments to be fitted in beforehand, Charles might well have chosen this moment to give up his racing ambitions. Instead, with his sights still set on the Sandown Cup, Charles entered a horse whose name was unfortunately not to match his performance: Good Prospect.

The race, held rather ominously on Friday, 13 February, was attended by the Queen Mother, Princess Margaret and Diana. Racing fit at 11 stone 7 lb, Charles rode out to cheers from racegoers and soared over the first few fences. Alas, at the eighteenth fence Good Prospect jumped badly, pitching the Prince out of the saddle. Diana and his family were relieved to see Charles come back safely, albeit with a bloody nose. He went on to finish the season, riding the Queen Mother's horse Upton Grey at Newmarket in May, though not before he had hit the ground again at Cheltenham. In 1988 Prince Charles celebrated his first win as a racehorse owner with Devil's Elbow; but he has now given up his appearances as a jockey.

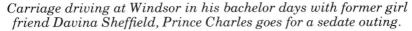

Carriage driving at Windsor in his bachelor days with former girl friend Davina Sheffield, Prince Charles goes for a sedate outing.

Prince Charles's first African safari in 1971 was a formative experience. He later returned with his mentor, Laurens van der Post.

If the Princess of Wales never feels entirely at ease on a horse, the problem goes back to her early days when she lost confidence. No one was more surprised than Charles to hear that she had suddenly turned out with the Belvoir Hunt when staying in Lincolnshire with her sister, Lady Sarah McCorquodale. Although she only went at a gentle pace, the experiment has not been repeated. Nevertheless, when the news got out she became the target for a storm of criticism from the anti-hunting brigade.

Prince Charles is not the only one who would like to see the beautiful Princess of Wales out riding with the same style and grace she brings to other activities. Encouraged by the Queen, and by her sister-in-law the Duchess of York, Diana sometimes goes riding at Sandringham or Balmoral – although she never looks a very happy member of the party. All the same, people who know her would not be surprised if one day she accompanied her two young sons on horseback. Many young mothers who, for one reason or another, have given up riding, or who have never ridden before, make the effort to go riding with their children.

William and Harry are already keen riders. Prince William is particularly fearless – too fearless, perhaps, for his mother's peace of mind. She makes a point of supervising her son's lessons, leads out the ponies, and makes every effort to encourage their natural love of riding. No one was more proud than Diana when William won a rosette at his first pony show.

The little Princes are given lessons by the girl groom at Highgrove, Marilyn Cox. At the age of four Prince William started on Smokey, a Shetland pony on loan from Princess Anne. Shetlands make an ideal first pony except for one thing: they have a highly developed interest in snatching a mouthful of juicy grass whenever possible. With this in mind, Smokey has been given a string which runs from his bit through to his brow-band to discourage him from taking a quick snack and catapulting his young rider over his ears.

A little later, the rapidly growing Prince William was promoted to a Welsh mountain pony called Llanerch Topaz, a gift from the Welsh Pony and Cob Society. Just under 12 hands, Topaz has made an excellent second-stage pony for William: responsive, but with no Bandit-like tricks such as standing up on his hind legs. Meanwhile, Harry has inherited Smokey. Their ponies travel from Highgrove in horseboxes to Balmoral for the summer holiday and to Sandringham for the royal family's New Year break.

Smaller animals have their place in the royal affections too – the young Princes keep hamsters at home. Asked one day if she read the tabloid newspaper the *Sun*, the Princess of Wales replied; 'I don't read it. I use it as bedding for my children's pet hamsters.'

William and Harry have been brought up to be careful both of their pets and of any equipment. As a child, Prince Charles once mislaid a dog lead at Sandringham to the annoyance of the Queen, who sent him to look for it. 'Dog leads cost money,' she explained.

One of Prince Charles's headline-hitting comments also concerned dogs. It was made in 1969, when he was invested as Prince of Wales and making a tour of the Principality. At a local craft fair, an artist making drawings of dogs remarked to him that she should be drawing corgis. 'You could have knocked me down with a Prince of Wales feather,' the artist said later, because Prince Charles had replied, 'I don't like corgis. I like labradors.'

The corgi-world was stunned, especially as the Queen had given him a Pembrokeshire corgi called Whisky, son of her dearly loved Sugar, for an eighth birthday present. However, the Prince of Wales makes up his own mind on these matters, and the first dog he brought to his own home was a black labrador called Harvey, named in memory of his favourite childhood rabbit.

The Prince now has one particular animal-friend. She is small, smart, and boasts a brown and white fur coat. She answers to the name of Tigger. She is a Jack Russell bitch, and popular with the whole family.

At Highgrove, Prince Charles has taken a recent interest in breeding National Hunt horses. His mare, Spartan Legacy, has produced several good foals. Among them is a filly called Amethea, for whom he has high hopes.

At nearby Broadfield Farm, recently bought by Prince Charles, he practises what he preaches by way of the gospel of organic farming. He also keeps a herd of dairy cows and a flock of sheep there.

The peace and tranquillity of the beautiful garden at Highgrove make it the perfect place for the whole family to relax away from the public eye. A few hundred yards from the house is the walled garden, restored to Prince Charles's own design, full of home-grown vegetables. In the huge greenhouses grow the scented plants which the Princess always has in the house.

The garden is a paradise for children. William and Harry have a pet rabbit which lives by the swimming pool, and beyond the swimming pool are the stables. The Sultan of Oman presented the Prince and Princess with a dovecote, which stands at the far end of the garden. Earlier, the violinist Yehudi Menuhin gave them a pond full of carp as a wedding present.

With its border of wild flowers, the garden is a sanctuary for butterflies in addition to tiny wild creatures which inhabit this rural setting. Not for Highgrove are the pesticides which have resulted in the destruction of many insects on which other species thrive. Among these are the beautiful barn owl, on whose behalf Prince Charles has been battling. Saving the barn owl is only one of his campaigns, but it is part of his very great desire to conserve the environment.

Prince Charles has gone on record as saying, 'I have this thing about wanting to do things well.' It is a philosophy that is particularly appropriate to the hard-driving game of polo, which sometimes breaks up the summer weekends at Highgrove. Ever since he was given a skewbald pony named Pecas at the age of twenty-one, Charles has found that, if there was one recreation that gave him total escape from the tensions of his high-pressure job, polo was it.

It was about seventeen years ago that the Queen began breeding the polo ponies from which Prince Charles is fortunate enough to have his choice. The first one to establish the royal line was a mare called Mayling, bred by Lord Mountbatten. In 1963, Mayling produced a filly called Mayfly who went on to foal two of Prince Charles's favourites: Mayfair, born in 1977, and Samphire, born in 1979. Lord Mountbatten, Prince Charles's mentor, would have been delighted that his original mare has proved to be such an excellent founder of the line.

Prince Charles was fifteen before he was allowed to play in practice matches on the Guards' Club grounds at Smith's Lawn at Windsor, usually in a team captained by Prince Philip. Now he plays what is

Highlight of the Bertram Mills circus for Prince Charles and his sister Princess Anne as teenagers, was their meeting with a four-week-old lion cub.

known as 'High Goal' polo. This refers to a system of handicapping. Polo players are handicapped in an ascending order of merit from minus two to a maximum of ten. With a handicap of four, Prince Charles is in the top echelon of British players. Only about ten per cent of the 660-odd players in twenty-four official clubs have handicaps of three and above. All the same, Prince Charles still has a little way to go before he beats the handicap of five which his father achieved in the 1960s.

One of the most important people in Prince Charles's polo career has been Major Ronald Ferguson, father of the Duchess of York. As Prince Charles's polo manager, Major Ferguson organizes most aspects of the Prince's polo season. Another polo VIP is his stud groom, Raul Correa. Born in Argentina, Correa usually dresses in South American style with a sombrero and a gaucho belt; he supervises the care of the Prince's string of ten polo ponies. At Windsor, the ponies are taken in from wintering out at grass at the end of February, and then brought to a peak of fitness with plenty of hard galloping and special attention to diet. A polo pony must be able to turn and stop immediately when required, and it takes seven years to train one properly.

Prince Charles's fondness for his polo ponies is quite obvious to spectators at Windsor. He brings sugar for the ponies, and when his

At the age of seven, Prince Charles was less keen on riding than his sister. At the West Norfolk Hunt near Sandringham, he is happy to take charge of a stray hound.

two little sons are there they are shown how to coax a pony into taking a lump of sugar from their hands. Contrary to what has been said about the Princess disliking polo, she has gone on record to say that she enjoys the game. She is knowledgeable about the play, and explains what is happening to Prince William – who continually asks how Daddy is getting on.

It has sometimes been said that because the Princess of Wales does not own a pet of her own she is not interested in animals. But Diana shares Prince Charles's love of country life, where dogs and horses are a natural part of the family background. Also, she shares her children's excitement when they are introduced to new animals on trips and at shows.

One explanation for Diana not owning a pet is that she cares too much: she suffers terribly when an animal dies. She still remembers the feeling of devastation she experienced as a child when her pet guinea pig died, only a few months after she began caring for it. She was well able to understand William and Harry's feelings when they were terribly upset by the death of two favourite dogs, one a guard dog at Kensington Palace, the other Princess Anne's Lurcher, Laura.

From that day in July 1981 when Charles and Diana left Buckingham Palace in the State Landau for their honeymoon, drawn by six of the famous Windsor Greys, it has been evident that theirs was to be a family life which had a lot of room for animals.

8

THE PRINCESS ROYAL
AND MARK PHILLIPS

'Even if you do have a bit of a barney,
by the time you get back to the stables it's either
made sense or it hasn't.'

The Queen's only daughter, born in 1950, was to outshine her three brothers in the world of competitive horsemanship. Princess Anne and Prince Charles took riding lessons on the same pony, an Irish strawberry roan named William, which became such a pet that he once walked into the schoolroom at Windsor and shared their tea. Anne was two and a half when she was first lifted on to William's back. Sybil Smith, famous for always riding side-saddle in Hyde Park's Rotten Row, gave the Princess her first lessons. Two years younger than Prince Charles, who had already learned to trot, the Princess had to be restrained from urging her pony on to a gallop at the first lesson.

Unknown to her at the time, a small boy called Mark Phillips sat on his first pony – a Shetland called Tiny Wee – at the age of eighteen months. These two determined children were mad about horses from the start, and that aspect of their lives was to share a similar pattern. On the Phillips' farm near Tewkesbury in the heart of the Gloucestershire countryside, it was Mark's mother who gave her son his early riding lessons. When his younger sister Sarah inherited Tiny Wee, Mark went on to a pony of 11 hands called Longdon Beauty.

'Beauty probably had a very great influence on Mark,' Mrs Phillips once remarked. 'She was a pony that when he kicked, she went; and when he pulled the reins, she stopped. But she was a very lively lady – there might be a pheasant jumping out of the hedge, or anything – so he had to anticipate – think ahead.' From the first, Mrs Phillips would not allow her children to use a stick. She had her own philosophy: 'I really do believe that it's the pony that makes the child – not the other way around – so we always attempted to buy him the best ponies within our means.'

The Queen was also extremely painstaking when it came to choosing ponies for young Charles and Anne. After William came Greensleeves, a Welsh mare, followed by Bandit, a Welsh grey – both duly passed down from big brother to little sister. Princess Anne's first pony of her own was High Jinks, a twelfth birthday present from the Queen. A smart bay, 11 hands high, High Jinks went with Princess

Anne to Benenden School in Kent, where he was kept nearby at Moat House stables. She would rise early to fit in a seventy-five-minute lesson under the supervision of Cherry Kendall, who had been a successful competitor at the Three Day Badminton Horse Trials.

Princess Anne had already won a first prize at an Ascot gymkhana and entered several junior competitions where her parents had a chance to observe her future prowess. On 21 April 1965, Princess Anne gave her mother a birthday present in the shape of a red rosette, awarded for her horsemanship in the Garth Hunt Pony Club hunter trials.

Her interest in hunters was to lead to her first recorded fall. Out with the Oxford University Draghounds at Shotover Park, her horse fell at the last fence – a hedge with a rail on the top. The Princess seemed shaken and was taken back to the house by the Master of the Draghounds, who had no idea until later that she had been injured. In fact she had broken her nose, which was later operated on, but she made little fuss about the incident.

Many young pony-lovers can be put off by a bad fall, but as any first-class rider will tell you, it is impossible to reach the top without coming a few croppers. Having broken her nose at the age of fifteen, Princess Anne chipped a bone in her shoulder and suffered painful bruising when competing in the European Championships at Kiev. At the Montreal Olympic Games of 1967, she fell in the cross-country event and suffered severe concussion.

Mark Phillips, who has taken part in four Olympics and is the only rider to have won the Badminton championship four times, recently revealed his own catalogue of damages: 'I have broken my arm a couple of times and once had quite bad concussion. I lost the sight of my right eye for twenty-four hours. My foot got squashed a few years ago and I've also got a compressed disc in my spine. I'm starting to crack up a bit!'

Princess Anne has repeatedly fallen and just as often gone right back into the saddle – sometimes covered in water or mud from a missed water jump. Through courage and stamina as well as natural talent, both she and her husband have won the admiration of riders and horse-lovers far beyond their own family circle.

It was in 1968 that Alison Oliver was asked for an impartial opinion on the Princess's potential as a competitive rider. Mrs Oliver was then one of the foremost instructors in the country, and Princess Anne was accepted at Brookfield Farm, her training stables at Warfield in Berkshire, only after rigorous testing of her skills. Mrs Oliver had to satisfy herself about the ability and potential of all intending pupils, no matter who they were. A strong sense of commitment was another

One of the world's leading horse trial riders, Princess Anne awaits her turn on Hatton Springs, while her daughter Zara Phillips takes in the equestrian scene on Tango.

Aptly called Tango, Zara Phillips' pony is a spirited ride. The latest in a long line of royal horsewomen, Zara shapes up to the family tradition by taking part in the Windsor Horse Trials.

essential quality, and Mrs Oliver also stipulated that the horse must match the rider.

Princess Anne and Doublet proved to be a perfect combination. The little chestnut given to her by the Queen for her twentieth birthday was probably Anne's favourite horse. He was also a challenge: 'He was undoubtedly the quickest stopper I've ever come across,' she commented. This meant that she was frequently to be seen disappearing over his head. But relishing a challenge, the Princess began a routine of intensive schooling at Warfield.

Now an important member of the 'family firm', as the royals call themselves, Princess Anne also had a demanding job to do. The only way of combining her equestrian ambitions with royal duties was to get up at the crack of dawn to put in a good two hours' practice at the Oliver stables. Afterwards she would return to the Palace, bath and change, ready for a full working day. This is a routine she has pursued ever since. Although the journey from Gatcombe Park in Gloucestershire takes at least an hour and a half, Princess Anne will usually have had a workout on one of her horses before arriving at her office in Buckingham Palace to check over the day's forthcoming events.

Meanwhile, Mark Phillips had proved his abilities as a sportsman, playing rugby and cricket for his school and breaking the high jump record. But as with Anne, riding took over. His family had moved to a farm in Wiltshire and Mark represented the local Beaufort Hunt Pony Club team for five years. As a result he was selected to train for three-day eventing. Unlike Princess Anne, whom he first met in 1968 at a Buckingham Palace party given for the British Olympic team, he did not have to contend with press photographers letting off their flash bulbs just as he approached a jump. Being royal was in fact the greatest single disadvantage she faced in her early years as a competitive rider. 'When I'm approaching a water jump with dozens of photographers waiting for me to fall in, the horse is the only one who doesn't know I'm royal,' she later commented drily.

After a gruelling twelve months dividing her time between official duties and entering qualifying competitions, Princess Anne's first Badminton lay ahead. The annual Three Day Event is, along with the Burghley Horse Trials, the goal of every advanced rider. At the Rushall Horse Trials in March 1971 she competed on Doublet against Mark Phillips, who won brilliantly on his eight-year-old Great Ovation. The European Three Day Event Championship at Burghley

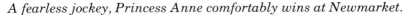

A fearless jockey, Princess Anne comfortably wins at Newmarket.

A keen judge of dogs as well as horses, Princess Anne accompanied by Baskerville at the Army Horse Trials at Tidworth.

had also brought Mark and Anne together in the lists of competitors. This time the results were reversed, and the Queen had the great happiness of being able to present the Raleigh Trophy, a gold medal and a cheque to her winning daughter.

Badminton is a severe test of both horse and rider. Three main skills are involved: dressage, cross-country racing and showjumping. The difficult course includes a notorious lake, the scene of many a ducking.

At Badminton that year Princess Anne was again on Doublet, competing against tremendous odds among the top-class riders. The South American-bred horse and his blonde rider had a tremendous start when they led the twenty-five entrants in the dressage section. The next day, Mark Phillips got ahead of her, keeping the lead across the thirty-three fences in the cross-country, while Princess Anne dropped to fourth place on timing. On the third day, Doublet's hind leg splashed the water while jumping, bringing her down to fifth place. Mark Phillips was the winner, but it was Princess Anne who was the first to congratulate him.

Named as BBC Sports Personality of the Year, Sportswoman of 1971 by the *Daily Express*, and recipient of the Sportswriters' Award of that year, Princess Anne and Doublet shared their success with millions of enthusiasts watching them on television. Had Doublet been a nervous horse, worried by the pressmen, things might have gone less well. As it was, she was preparing him for the following year's Olympics. Together they had proved their nerve.

Nor were success and happiness limited to the professional sphere. Romance had blossomed. After Badminton Mark Phillips partnered Princess Anne on the dance floor at the Duke and Duchess of Beaufort's victory dinner at Badminton House.

Since their first meeting in 1968 they had seen each other at three-day events, at house parties and, more recently, at Sandringham and Balmoral, where Mark was invited to bring his labrador and join the shooting parties. Legend has it that when Mark first asked his mother if he could bring Princess Anne to dinner at Great Somerford, Anne Phillips was surprised to learn that her son knew the Princess's telephone number. They seemed just part of a group of friends which included the rider Richard Meade, whom many thought was Princess Anne's foremost suitor.

Fully aware of the privileges of being able-bodied and endowed with the stamina to realize her ambitions, Princess Anne became patron of what was to be one of her favourite charities: the Riding for the Disabled Association. In assisting less fortunate children to learn to ride she shared the obvious joy that riding brings to the physically and mentally disabled. The idea proved enormously popular, and now owners all over the country offer their services and their ponies to local organizations.

After the successes of 1971, Princess Anne had every justification in cherishing dreams of being selected for the Munich Olympic team. But the following year her luck seemed to have turned. Just before Badminton Doublet sprained a tendon, and the Princess was forced to withdraw. The injury put an end to his competitive career.

With her Olympic hopes dashed, Princess Anne and Alison Oliver set about preparing a horse called Columbus for the challenge of defending her European Championship title. The partnership was not to succeed. The Queen's big and powerful grey was a handful and on the steeplechase course he proved too much for her, forcing her to withdraw. While Mark took over Columbus for a time, Princess Anne tried out Mark's horse, Persian Holiday.

Although Mark had not had to cope with the publicity which attended Princess Anne's every mishap, he had experienced many challenges and certainly a lot more tempestuous horses than Princess Anne was likely to come across. While waiting to enter the army, he came into the possession of Rock On, a 16.1 hands gelding who was described as 'wild as a horse could possibly be'. On the credit side the horse was affectionate, and had speed combined with great courage.

Horse and rider went for schooling to north Devon, where the colourful three-day event rider, Bertie Hill, really made them slog it out. At the Crookham Horse Trials Rock On won the novice section, but his rider lost his four front teeth. Mark simply shoved the teeth back in place and finished the course. Short-sighted, he had also recently begun to wear contact lenses – spectacles are a disadvantage to the cross-country rider.

Rock On had cost only £400; once trained, he proved a successful horse. Mark competed on him in Ireland, and then in Normandy for the European Championships. After winning the 1972 Badminton title on Cheers, he had two well-trained horses with potential. Then, shortly before Burghley, disaster struck in the form of a road accident. When he opened the trailer to see how the horses were, 'Rock On shot out of the back like a champagne cork', according to Mark's description, and was later found a quarter of a mile away in a pub car park. Neither horse was fit to ride at Burghley. Instead, he took on Great Ovation, who, though he was a quality horse, had some defects.

After riding him at Burghley, Mark said, 'Great Ovation wasn't the most generous horse in my life, and the one thing I could never do in any championship was to jump a corner, because he'd always run out.' Despite this problem, which dropped Mark to fifth place at Burghley, skilled horsemanship and a continuing battle of wills enabled him to win the Badminton Trophy for two successive years on Great Ovation. But at Burghley that year, it was Princess Anne on Doublet who won the individual title.

In 1972, their roles were reversed again. Mark qualified for the Munich Olympics but Anne – now minus Doublet – did not. The British team won a gold medal, supported by a wildly cheering Princess Anne who was accompanied by an equally enthusiastic Queen of England.

In September 1973, just before her wedding, it was all change once more as Anne went to Kiev in the USSR with an all-female team for the European Championships. Mark, who with his fiancé's father was among the spectators, saw her fall at the most difficult fence on the course, which claimed some thirty other victims.

Describing the incident later, Princess Anne said,

> It was like hitting tarmac as far as I was concerned. I had never hit the ground as hard or as fast . . . from mid-thigh to mid-calf; I couldn't feel a thing. I wasn't, at that stage, aware that there was anything wrong with my shoulder – but I couldn't walk – I could stand on one leg, that was about all. Goodwill looked completely stunned and I couldn't walk so I decided that there wasn't a great deal of point in going on.

Prince Philip, who had accompanied the team in his capacity as President of the International Equestrian Federation, was impatient

Left, *Ready to ride anything, Princess Anne masters the swaying gait of a camel in Quartar.*

Below, *Princess Anne's tours on behalf of the Save the Children Fund achieve the sort of publicity money cannot buy. Here on a visit to Kenya, she was pictured with a leopard cub in the Nairobi Game Park.*

to hurry his daughter back home for X-rays – but Princess Anne, anxious to learn more about Goodwill's condition, visited him in his stables before agreeing to go back to her Moscow hotel room.

If he was daunted by the sudden change from being a private individual to becoming an associate member of the Royals, he had no hesitation in telling an interviewer: 'If that thought had stopped me from marrying the person I loved, it wouldn't have been much of a relationship.' With the same authority that he had applied to his army life and career in competitive sports, Mark had qualified.

Although top-calibre riders are generally at pains to disguise a sentimental side, Mark frankly demonstrated the emotion he felt when he lost Rock On, possibly one of his finest partners in eventing. After the car accident Rock On had needed an operation, and had died while coming round from the anaesthetic. Mark made no attempt to hide the emotion he felt at the time:

> I cried and cried and cried. Even now, just talking about him gives me a funny feeling. . . . He was the bravest horse I ever knew, and you have to admire pure courage in a horse. He'd look at you with big, wide, brown eyes and I'd think. . . . Why should you be so brave, so courageous?

In 1974, less than a year after her marriage, Princess Anne was to go through what she afterwards described as the worst day in her life when her faithful friend Doublet died under traumatic circumstances. After the injury which put him out of showjumping, the spirited little horse whom Anne adored was kept at Windsor. He was always pleased to see her and keen for exercise, so she continued to ride him at a gentle pace whenever opportunity allowed. Their last ride together was at Smith's Lawn, Windsor. Suddenly she heard a loud and terrifying crack. Numb with shock, she dismounted immediately to find that Doublet had broken a leg. The agonizing experience of holding her faithful friend as the vet gave him the painless injection which ended his life caused the Princess to break down with grief.

Many horses pass through the hands of a top-class competitor as he or she looks for the ideal partner. There is always one who means more than the rest. To Princess Anne, Doublet was that one above all.

Husband and wife – royal princess and army instructor – helped each other to train for their competitions. They are as open and forthright with their criticisms as they are supportive of each other's efforts. Mark said: 'Sometimes I don't know what the hell I'm doing wrong and I ask Princess Anne to see if she can put her finger on the problem.' On occasions her words could be quite pointed. On that subject, she once remarked: 'Even if you do have a bit of a barney, by the time you get back to the stables, it's either made sense or it hasn't, and the chances are that you've probably translated it into something useful.'

Mark and Peter Phillips.

After the terrifying ordeal of 1974 when there was a kidnap attempt on Princess Anne in the Mall, only a few hundred yards from Buckingham Palace, life was never to be the same. It resulted in a major security shake-up. Since then, even when riding in private competitions she is accompanied by plain-clothed detectives.

With the loss of Doublet, she now concentrated on bringing Goodwill into peak condition, setting her sights on the next Olympic Games, to be held in Montreal in 1976. In the 1975 European Championships in West Germany, they were rewarded with a silver medal. Only one other woman in the history of three-day eventing has won on two different horses in the European Championships, and Princess Anne was duly rewarded by being short-listed for the Olympic team. With Mark Phillips as reserve rider, husband and wife flew economy class to Montreal, where they shared similar accommodation to all the other competitors.

Princess Anne rode for an individual medal after two of the team members' horses had been eliminated, leaving only hers and Richard Meade's. Following her appearance in the dressage section, she entered the cross-country. Falling badly at the nineteenth fence, she was unconscious for a few minutes, but climbed back on to Goodwill and completed the course. These Olympics had meant a lot to her, and earlier she had stated her philosophy: 'Being on the short list I consider to be an achievement, and if I actually get round – that will be quite something.' Dazed with concussion, it really *had* been something to get round. She went on to the final day to complete the show-jumping, ending in twenty-fourth place. Princess Anne felt she had gone to Montreal for Britain, and she had to do her job there. Olympic riders are a tough breed.

With the 1976 Olympics behind them, the couple decided to make some major moves in their lives. Princess Anne was expecting her first child in November 1977, and Mark Phillips had decided to leave the army and earn his bread and butter as a farmer. Together they went househunting.

Gatcombe Park near Minchinhampton in Gloucestershire is a typical Cotswold estate. Surrounded by some 1200 acres of arable and pasture land, the house with its mellow front and portico sits at the head of the combe (or hill), with south-facing views. Built in 1720, it is certainly the least formal of all the royal residences, and reflects the easy-going atmosphere of Great Somerford rather than any of the houses in which Princess Anne was brought up. Dogs and green wellies are to be seen in the porch, there are flowered chintzes decorating the sitting room, and the feeling is that of a busy, comfortable farmhouse.

Almost a year's work was needed on the house and stables before they could move in. 'We did the thing you should never do; have a baby and move house at the same time,' commented Princess Anne, who ten days after the birth of her son, Peter, moved in with the house still unfinished. Columbus, their best horse at that time, was bedded down in a cowshed and the construction of a new stables with fifteen loose boxes was a priority. Built to their own plans was a 'swimming pool' for the horses; important in the treatment of the swellings and injuries to which thoroughbred horses are prone, exercise in water is a modern technique. Princess Anne and her husband are both expert in the care of their horses, and keeping them fit is a matter of close and continual concern. Soon to join Columbus in the modern stable complex were Persian Minstrel, a brown gelding from Devon which was nicknamed Smudge, and Frog Prince, a newly broken three-year-old which promised great talent and was given the stable name of Toad.

But Gatcombe was intended first and foremost to be a proper, working, profitable farm. During his first year there, Mark attended Cirencester Agricultural College to learn all he could about modern techniques in farming. When free from official duties, Princess Anne lent a practical hand on the farm with harvesting and tractor driving.

For A-level geography at school she had studied agriculture and farming – useful knowledge for life at Gatcombe. Princess Anne's love of the countryside has always been strong. Whether opening a Young

Peter and Zara Phillips.

Farmers' club in the Midlands or inspecting land drains at a children's refugee camp in Africa, the practical knowledge she has accumulated often surprises people who do not expect a princess to be an expert on such subjects.

Gatcombe is a real home, and the family atmosphere would not be complete without an assortment of dogs. When the family first moved there Fox, Mark's labrador bred at the Sandringham kennels, was joined by Princess Anne's Dumfriesshire foxhound, a bitch called Pleasure, then two. Pleasure was to bring some problems. Mark commented that she was:

> one of the most intelligent dogs I've ever had the misfortune to meet. Her low cunning was almost unbelievable. At Gatcombe she became a great visitor – her round took in most of the neighbourhood. We'd try to stop her going off, but she'd wander out of the house as if she was only going to spend a penny, pretend to be sniffing about, doing nothing in particular, then she'd get to the corner – and be gone like a lamplighter. A few hours later, we'd get a phone call saying, 'We've got Pleasure – would you mind coming to pick her up.' And there she'd be, curled up in front of the fire being fed biscuits. She was so sweet, no one could bear to throw her out, so of course she always went back.

Then came Princess Anne's black labrador Moriarty, who also went missing at first, but after some training would come to heel nicely. Still plagued by Pleasure's disappearances, Mark thought of an ingenious method to put a stop to these outings by harnessing the two together, whistling to Moriarty to drag Pleasure home safely.

As the years passed, new dogs arrived. Pleasure died of a brain haemorrhage, and the Dumfriesshire Hunt offered Princess Anne another hound. She chose Random, a gentle dog which would crouch in the van when the other hounds were raring to join the Huntsman. At one time the Princess had a Gascony hound given to her by Sir Rupert Buchanan Jardine, Joint Master of the Dumfriesshire Hunt; Baskerville had a very good nose for vermin.

Mark also had a new dog, Laura – a lurcher. Lurchers are a hunting dog looking rather like a greyhound, fast on the ground and able to turn quickly. Unfortunately, Laura had to be put down in 1979 after an accident in the kennels at Balmoral. But in the royal family dogs and horses are often passed round from one member to another, according to their needs at the time. When Laura was put down the Queen gave her daughter a corgi puppy called Apollo.

Having been surrounded by corgis all her childhood, Princess Anne might not necessarily have acquired one for herself. But, remembering the long hours she used to spend teaching her corgi, Sherry, to jump through a hoop, she knew what lively and excellent companions the little Welsh cattle dogs make for children. By the time Zara Phillips appeared on the scene in 1981, Apollo was a firmly established member of the family. Apart from being a favourite with children, corgis are good house dogs and are not prone to stray.

Unlike the Queen and the Queen Mother, Princess Anne does not believe in keeping a whole pack of corgis, because problems can arise when you have several dogs of the same breed. For one thing, they are inclined to be more interested in each other and therefore more difficult to train. For another, jealousies often break out. This, unfortunately, proved all too true in the case of the labrador Moriarty. After one of his worst displays of jealousy when taken on a shoot in Yorkshire, Mark decided to retire him. Fox was promoted to top gun dog, while Moriarty enjoyed a happy retirement at the Phillips family home in Wiltshire, away from the competition.

With the new stables in working order at Gatcombe, Princess Anne and Mark Phillips wasted no time in re-establishing their riding careers. Mark turned his energies towards showjumping and in July 1978 gave a great performance at the Royal International in the famous King George V Gold Cup. In 1981 he won the Badminton Horse Trials for the fourth time.

Princess Anne had started teaching her son Peter to ride when he

Princess Anne rides to hounds.

was three, leading him out on his first pony, Smokey. When Peter went to boarding school, Smokey was handed on to the Prince of Wales's children. Shetland ponies like Smokey are long-lived, and often give faithful service to generations of children. Zara had been given a pony of her own in 1983 when she was two and a half. In 1989 Peter was riding Trigger, a ten-year-old Palomino.

Princess Anne was competing again within weeks of Zara's birth in May 1981. The Queen had a talented chestnut called Stevie B which she qualified for Burghley. But two-thirds of the way round the course, Stevie B tried to fly at the dangerous Trout Hatchery fence and instead fell into the water, giving his rider a ducking.

Five years later, at the age of thirty-five, she was to discover a new and exciting challenge when she appeared at Epsom as an amateur flat race jockey in a race sponsored by the Riding for the Disabled Association. Her participation naturally caused great interest, and over £60,000 was raised for the charity. Riding a horse called Against the Grain, she came in a very creditable fourth and soon won professional praise as she rode in further flat races. 'She has been an intelligent, quick-learning student under her mentor, the trainer David Nicholson,' wrote Danny Hall, racing editor of the *Daily*

Princess Anne riding in Windsor Great Park with Peter, 11, Zara, 7, and Prince William, 6.

Express, in August 1988. He was even more impressed by her two victories on Insular at York and Vayrua at Newmarket, which he described as 'models of brilliant pace judgement, worthy of champion jockey Steve Cauthen himself'. In the same year she took part in the Grand Military Meeting at Sandown Park as a jump jockey on Cnoc Na Cuille. Her husband, mother and grandmother were there as spectators.

No one in the world of competitive riding doubts Princess Anne's courage or stamina, but how do her family feel about her participation in a sport where life and limb are often at considerable risk? Said Mark Phillips, 'I've got confidence in her as a jockey and the horses she rides – so I just hope that the two of them can put it all together on the day. But I must admit I'm always glad when she comes back in one piece.'

Although horses are her hobby and her passion, Princess Anne has a job to do and her official duties come before anything else. Fully worthy of the title of Princess Royal bestowed on her by the Queen in 1987, the Princess manages to combine marriage, motherhood and a programme of over five hundred official engagements every year. She supports seventy-eight charities and works hard to justify her Civil List allowance out of which, like other members of the royal family, she has to pay her administrative staff, contribute towards official cars and cover the expenses incurred on royal visits. All the same, Princess Anne spends more time at Gatcombe than Prince Charles manages to do at Highgrove. Gatcombe is the Princess's base, and 'Must get home' is a phrase which the royal family have become accustomed to hearing from her.

Just as the Princess works hard at her official commitments, so Mark has to work to support his family. He now boosts his income as a farmer by lecturing at various equestrian seminars around the world: you can spend a weekend at a luxury hotel and hear Captain Phillips lecturing on the techniques of dressage, show-jumping and cross-country racing at Gleneagles.

He has also accepted sponsorship from the Range Rover company and developed a scheme which enables eighteen young riders to go to Gatcombe each year and receive specialized tuition. At the end of the course the most promising young rider receives a bursary of £1500. It was his idea to bring young riders to good horses, since he knows as well as anyone the importance of a well-matched partnership between horse and rider. By 1980 Range Rover were sponsoring a team of horses which included such thoroughbreds as Lincoln, Classic Lines, Fieldsman, Highwayman X, Town and Country, and Rough and Tough. At the 1981 Badminton, Mark received the Butler Bowl from the Queen's hands as leading British rider with his mount Lincoln. Later in the season Classic Lines won a place in the British team to compete at Hooge Mierde in the Netherlands.

With Range Rover sponsoring his horses, Mark and Anne developed plans for a new venture. In 1983, the gates of Gatcombe were opened to the public for the first time for a one-day horse trial, which has now become a popular annual event. Neighbours are roped in as stewards, and the children as helpers: Zara Phillips can be seen proudly displaying a red T-shirt bearing the slogan 'Gatcombe Park Horse Trials – Menial Tasks Division'.

Princess Anne is the first royal princess in nine hundred years to marry the man she wanted without having to consider either politics or status. She is also the only one to have ridden in the Olympics. Her outstandingly successful Save the Children Fund tour of Africa in 1982 not only helped to raise a record sum for charity, but established her as the most popular member of the royal family. Her strong, uncompromising character has been formed by a sport which demands a high degree of courage as well as mental and physical co-ordination. If their children, Peter and Zara Phillips, decide to enter the competitive arena of international horsemanship they will get the support from their parents. But they will have a hard act to follow.

9

THE QUEEN'S YOUNGER CHILDREN

'Horses, horses! I'm sick of hearing about them.
Can't you talk about anything else?'

In every horse-loving family there is usually one who does not react to their spell. In the royal family it is Prince Andrew who finds his sporting interests elsewhere. When he married Sarah Ferguson in 1986, the bride was as much at home on a horse as her mother-in-law the Queen or her sister-in-law the Princess Royal; but apart from a ceremonial appearance or two in the Mall, the bridegroom had hardly been seen on a horse since his childhood. The reason is simple: as a child he suffered from hay fever and developed an allergy to horses. Now he has got rid of the allergy, but he still leaves the riding to Sarah and to the rest of the royal family.

Before his marriage, Prince Andrew often described himself as a loner. People were puzzled as to how the Queen's handsome second son could refer to himself in these terms. Perhaps it had something to do with the fact that he so often found himself left out of the conversation in a family where talk frequently centres around horseflesh. Horse talk is second nature to Sarah, but it has been known to irritate Andrew. Once, during a visit to Cowes, he joined a group of people only to find they were discussing the merits of various hunters. Andrew exploded in exasperation: 'Horses, horses! I'm sick of hearing about them. Can't you talk about anything else?'

Not that horses haven't played a significant part in Prince Andrew's childhood, adolescence and courtship – far from it. No member of the royal family can grow up far removed from the calendar of equine events.

Andrew and Sarah first met, in fact, behind the ponylines at Windsor. 'Doesn't everyone meet at polo?' asked Sarah's mother Susan in a now famous remark which highlighted the charmed circle around the royal family into which Sarah was born. One of Sarah's first memories is playing at the end of a cord held by a grown-up so she did not wander on to the Guards' Club polo ground where her father, Major Ronald Ferguson, was thundering up and down. A team mate of Prince Philip's, and later polo manager to Prince Charles, Major Ferguson was dubbed Polo-Stick in Waiting by the Queen. Sarah and her sister used to watch their father playing polo at Windsor; and it was here that they met the royal children who had come to watch *their* father. Smith's Lawn at Windsor was Sarah's original stamping ground; and

A sturdy toddler, Prince Andrew was brought up with the royal corgis but chose a terrier to give to his wife.

the Fergusons' house at nearby Sunningdale was open house to all players during the polo season.

Some fifteen years later, with Andrew in the Navy and Sarah having moved into a jet-setting crowd, their paths might not have crossed again had it not been for Royal Ascot, when it was the Queen's turn to hold open house at Windsor Castle. So when the coveted invitation in the large square envelope with the royal cipher arrived, Sarah accepted. Fate, in the shape of Sarah's good friend the Princess of Wales who had wangled the invitation, was to bring Andrew and Sarah together again. Sarah, a non-stop chatterbox who had no difficulty fitting in to the royal background, found herself well matched with the teasing Prince who tried to force-feed her on chocolate profiteroles while she was meant to be dieting. 'You haven't changed,' she told him. Nor, as a matter of fact, had Sarah.

Despite his later aversion to horses, as a small boy Andrew had been an enthusiastic visitor to the Royal Mews at Windsor. Accompanied by a favourite labrador called Francis, and Sherry, a third-generation corgi, Andrew would go along with one of the grooms to inspect the horses. Afterwards he would have a long session with his own pony, a miniature Shetland called Valkyrie.

No more than 36 inches high, Valkyrie was a typically shaggy version of the breed. Andrew was genuinely fond of all the horses in the Mews and, although never particularly keen to ride, took a deep interest in Valkyrie's care and grooming. He learned how to tie her up using the quick release knot for the halter rope, how to clean out her tiny hooves, and how to put her tack on. Having done all this with the help of a stable groom, Andrew would proudly lead the little pony out, all correctly saddled and bridled. The curious thing – according to the royal horse expert Judith Campbell, who spent much time at the Windsor Mews when Andrew was a small boy – was that he then seemed interested only in returning Valkyrie to her stable and helping to unharness her again.

For several years Andrew refused to be parted from Valkyrie. She was so small that she could travel in a box as freight, and was taken by train to Balmoral in a large wooden crate. Andrew would sometimes go out on his Shetland with the Queen riding her favourite mare Betsy, but he preferred other amusements. Valkyrie was amenable to any sort of fun and games and obligingly trundled Andrew round in a miniature donkey barouche that had been made for Queen Victoria's children in 1846.

When he finally outgrew Valkyrie and the donkey cart Andrew was given Mr Dinkum, a pony which had belonged to Princess Anne. Even if he never took to horse riding – and it was some years before his allergy was discovered – it was considered essential that Andrew

The Duke and Duchess of York in Mauritius with a tame frigate bird.

The Duchess cuddling a koala bear in Brisbane, Australia.

should learn to be a competent horseman. For a time he was given lessons on Bandit, Prince Charles's old pony. But by the time Andrew went to boarding school other recreations, such as boxing and sailing, had claimed his interest. Unlike Charles, who took to polo at the age of thirteen, Prince Andrew's interest in riding had gone on the wane.

Twenty months older than Andrew, Sarah Ferguson had no such inhibitions about horses. Put on a Shetland called Nigger almost before she could walk, she soon went on to a larger pony – a grey called Peanuts.

Lessons were provided by her mother, and by the time she was ten Sarah's bedroom wall was covered with rosettes from gymkhanas and shows. Susan, who also gave lessons to some of Sarah's school friends, has described her younger daughter as 'one of the most natural riders you could ever hope to find. I could put her on anything and say – right, go ahead and jump that – and she did.'

At Lowood, the white-painted house in Sunningdale where Sarah spent her early days, there were always dogs. Her mother had eight: a labrador, three Irish wolfhounds, three basset hounds and Solly the pekinese, who was Sarah's childhood pet. It was a household strongly addicted to animals, in which horses played a major part.

Sarah's father was the fourth generation of his family to serve in the Life Guards, and had started playing polo when he joined the army in 1949. After his father died in 1966, leaving Dummer Down House in Hampshire and 800 acres of land to him as his only son, Ronald Ferguson left the army. When he was appointed Deputy Chairman of the Guards Polo Club at Windsor, the prospect of combining polo with farming seemed to Major Ferguson the perfect way of life.

In young adulthood, both Andrew and Sarah started to travel. Sarah explored America by Greyhound bus, continuing south to Argentina to see her mother, now divorced from her father and married to an Argentinian polo player. She visited her married sister Jane in Australia several times, and ended up working as a chalet girl in Switzerland.

In Australia she helped to herd cattle and went pig-hunting, and watched the soaring flight of the flocks of wild parrots. But there were less attractive aspects to the animal life of the Antipodes – Jane had warned her sister that snakes often found their way into the outside lavatory, known as the 'dunny'. Sarah, like many people, has always had a fear of snakes, and her phobia was not helped by Jane's account of the occasion when a deadly tiger snake had wriggled into the drawing room and concealed itself under the sofa.

Andrew, for his part, had already demonstrated at Gordonstoun that he was the rugged, outdoor type. Mad about flying, he had had his

The Queen and the Duchess of York ride out together.

first lessons there and had later graduated to gliding and parachute jumping. He accompanied his parents on a visit to Zambia, where he toured national parks and game reserves, and then spent two terms at a school in Canada before entering the Royal Naval College at Dartmouth. After being commissioned into the Royal Navy he served as a helicopter pilot, and saw action in the Falklands Conflict.

Home on leave with his family, Andrew went shooting at Sandringham with his father. He had been taken shooting by Prince Philip from a young age, and had shown a special interest in working the gun dogs which scent out, look for and pick up the game. Under the supervision of Prince Philip, many new techniques had been installed to conserve the game. There are now fourteen gamekeepers with the most modern devices to ward off poachers. Ferrets which seek out vermin underground are fitted with mini-transmitters to alert the gamekeepers to their whereabouts. And trip wires, causing 12-bore blanks to fire, had been installed to startle the poachers. As a result, bags went up from five thousand gamebirds in 1987 to nearly seven thousand in 1988. Even in 1984, when Prince Andrew was enjoying his leave, he would already have noticed a difference.

It would be hard to imagine a more romantic setting than Floors Castle in the Scottish Borders, where Andrew proposed to Sarah in

February 1986; the onion-shaped domes of the Castle seem to float enchantedly above the salmon-filled River Tweed. The formal announcement of the engagement came nearly a month later, and the couple were married in July.

With all the trappings of royal tradition, Andrew and Sarah, now Duke and Duchess of York, returned from their wedding at Westminster Abbey in the State Landau drawn by Windsor Greys, the four horses proudly decked out in gold ormolu harness and beautiful silver mane-dressings. It must also have been Major Ferguson's great day. Proudly escorting his daughter to the Abbey in the Glass Coach, last used when the Princess of Wales travelled to her wedding, the former Life Guards officer received a very special sign of recognition. The Queen had honoured Sarah Ferguson with a special escort of six cavalry troopers from the Life Guards. Resplendent in their plumes and breastplates, they clattered beside father and daughter on their way from Clarence House to the splendour of the royal wedding at Westminster Abbey.

Sarah's fierce loyalty is her outstanding characteristic. When certain allegations made in the press concerning her father's private life led to his departure from the Guards' Polo Club, Sarah gave him brave support. The Queen appreciates her second daughter-in-law's enormous qualities of goodwill, energy and enthusiasm, and they have many interests in common. These days Sarah is the Queen's regular riding companion; they often ride together on a couple of the Queen Mother's retired steeplechasers. Bringing a new zest to whatever she tackles, Sarah sometimes goes out carriage-driving Wells Fargo-style; her flame-coloured locks blow in the breeze as she drives the Queen's horses through the park at Windsor, seated in a black victoria.

Sarah's ability for tackling royal duties in characteristically active style has impressed the Queen. It seemed typical of the vigorous royal image when Sarah rode the Grand National winner Aldaniti through Windsor Great Park as part of a 250-mile sponsorship ride to raise money for the Bob Champion Cancer Trust, named after the jockey who rode the horse to victory after his amazing recovery from cancer. Sarah is involved in other charities, too. One of her first acts on becoming Duchess of York was to agree to be patron of the Blue Cross Animal Welfare Society, which cares for sick and needy animals.

Like Sarah, the Queen was once a naval wife and appreciates the problems of having no husband around for long spells at a time. When Sarah was pregnant with baby Beatrice, Andrew was transferred to the naval frigate HMS *Edinburgh* for a three-month voyage to Australia.

To ease the tedious months of waiting, Andrew had given her a puppy, the sailor's traditional parting gift to wife or girlfriend. Named

Above, *The Duchess of York with Bendicks, a Warwickshire terrier, a gift from Andrew before rejoining his ship.*

Right, *The Duchess carries baby Beatrice to her christening.*

Prince Edward (extreme right), has grown up with the labs and the corgis. Now they've been joined by the fluffy-tailed dorgis – the result of a cross between dachshunds and corgis. Taken at Balmoral Castle.

after the upmarket chocolate mints so popular with their owners, Bendicks – a Jack Russell terrier – was six months old at the time. Taken to polo matches, hugged, cuddled and exercised by his mistress, Bendicks became a minor celebrity in the months before the birth.

Jack Russells were originally trained to run with foxhounds and burrow into foxholes. But any burrowing that the bouncy Bendicks does in the future is likely to be in the gardens of the Duke and Duchess's new home, Sunninghill Park. Situated close to Windsor, it is not far from where Andrew spent much of his childhood and the house where Sarah was born. The plans for the Yorks' house have been the subject of contention. But close to Windsor, where Andrew spent so much of his childhood, and the comfortable family house at Sunningdale where Sarah was born, the finished result is certain to be a happy place where children, animals and friends will find a warm and welcoming atmosphere.

The Queen's children divide into two pairs: Prince Charles was followed two years later by Princess Anne; after a gap of ten years or so came Prince Andrew and then, in 1964, Prince Edward. Little was seen of Edward in public until his eighteenth birthday, when a delightful photograph was published showing him holding a black labrador called Frances from the Queen's Sandringham kennels. He was clearly a personable young man, firmly embedded in the traditional animal-loving mould of the Windsors.

Dubbed the 'Student Prince', he had distinguished himself by passing nine O-levels – a greater academic achievement than any other member of his immediate family – and was then attending Jesus College, Cambridge. As the youngest member of the family he has fewer demands made on him to appear in public as a member of the 'family firm'. 'He is a working man, you know,' a friend said when asked whether Prince Edward had attended Ascot. Edward, now involved in the theatre, had his own job to do.

Like his father and eldest brother, he has realized that conservation is a vital issue in the modern world. Wildcats are disappearing from the Braemar region near Balmoral, and has involved himself with a project to help re-establish them. He has also become committed to the movement to save the rainforests. Speaking at a function in aid of the World Wide Fund for Nature's RainForest Appeal, the Prince drew attention to the fact that the rainforests which provide the habitat for such animals as the bush buck, warthog, hyena, lion and leopard, as well as the almost extinct rhino, are seriously under threat. Unsparing with some horrific examples of the way in which these animals are driven to survive under deteriorating conditions, he made a clear and forceful impression on the audience, describing the destruction of the rainforests as 'one of the most frightening examples of man's total disregard for his natural habitat'.

In his private life, Prince Edward has shown himself to be not particularly interested in becoming part of the polo or hunting set. He enjoys riding for its own sake, as a form of exercise and relaxation. He doesn't

Prince Edward on his Eighteenth birthday at Sandringham.

*Making a rare appearance in the competition ring, Prince Edward
takes part in the Windsor Horse Show.*

own a horse of his own; when at Windsor, he uses one from the Mews.

Prince Edward rides well and has hunted a little, though his way of
life hardly allows him to participate in the vigorous feats of horsemanship which appeal to his eldest brother, Charles. He sometimes
rides with the Queen, or with his sister-in-law, the Duchess of York.
On her few excursions out riding, the Princess of Wales is said to feel
most confident with Prince Edward as an escort: she knows she can
rely on him not to go galloping ahead.

At Sandringham Prince Edward now hosts his own shooting parties,
and is rated a good shot. The Queen loans him the secluded Wood Farm
three miles from Sandringham House, as a base to entertain friends at
weekends.

Twenty-five in March 1989 and fifth in line to the throne, Prince
Edward is now Britain's most eligible bachelor. Speculation is rife
about which young lady will become the bride of the decade in the
1990s. One knowledgeable member of his inner circle commented:
'Whoever she proves to be you may be sure that she will be a girl who
loves the British countryside. She will be spending many an hour
gazing skyward at the birds when Prince Edward takes stock of
grouse, partridge, or pheasants overhead.'

10
THE ROYAL COUSINS

When asked on *Desert Island Discs* what
luxury she would take with her as a castaway,
Princess Michael replied: 'A cat.'

The Kent and Gloucester families today are the descendants of two of George VI's brothers, the Duke of Kent and the Duke of Gloucester. Their children, the present Duke of Kent, Princess Alexandra and Prince Michael, and the present Duke of Gloucester, are all first cousins of the Queen.

Apart from a love of animals, one other quality shared by the royal family is a highly developed sense of humour. They love it when something unexpected happens, especially when the tension of some formal event is broken by the appearance of an animal on the scene. The Duke and Duchess of Kent are a particularly natural and outgoing couple, and the spontaneous part played by a dog when they made an official trip to Jersey led to the sort of story which always amuses the Queen when it travels back to her.

The visit to Jersey had been organized with great formality. Met by the Governor's venerable Daimler at the airport, the Duke and Duchess were taken straight to Government House, where guests had been summoned to a dignified reception. The Governor and his wife had recently acquired a black labrador called Hannah. Although house-trained, Hannah was not yet ready to meet polite society on a grand scale and had been shut away in a back room. As so often happens with lively dogs, however, Hannah managed to get out. She bounded happily into the main salon where the Governor was making the customary small talk with the Duke and Duchess. At that point a butler entered, pushing a trolley laden with dainty sandwiches. Hannah's moment had come. She bounded up to the trolley and scoffed every sandwich in a few eager gulps. Whatever else she did, Hannah certainly put an end to the atmosphere of formality, and both Duke and Duchess broke into gales of laughter.

The incident seemed particularly to amuse the Duchess, who grew up in the Yorkshire countryside, where rumbustious labradors are not only tolerated but admired. Born Katharine Worsley, the Duchess spent her happy childhood in the heart of the glorious countryside filmed in the TV series *All Creatures Great and Small*. Her brother, Sir Marcus Worsley, once explained his own approach to the training of labradors: his are affectionate without losing character, and obedient without being stodgy. In short, he appreciates a dog which is a character; so does the royal family.

Edward, Duke of Kent, was the son of the exquisite Princess Marina of Greece and Prince George, Duke of Kent, fourth son of King George V. The death of the Duke in World War II left Princess Marina with three small children: Edward was six, his sister Alexandra five and their baby brother Michael only seven months old. Brought up at a rambling farmhouse in Buckinghamshire, all three children learned to ride. Their favourite dogs were chows.

After leaving Sandhurst the young Duke became a professional soldier, joining the Royal Scots Greys. He retired from the regiment in 1976 but, an excellent horseman, still rides in the Trooping the Colour almost every year. The Kents have three children: the Earl of St Andrews, Lady Helen Windsor and Lord Nicholas Windsor.

After living for seventeen years at Anmer Hall, a grace-and-favour residence on the Queen's Sandringham estate, the Duke and Duchess bought a former vicarage in Oxfordshire. With the happy atmosphere of a family home, the Victorian house has a swimming pool, tennis court and stables in the grounds.

On the Norfolk coast near Anmer Hall is a seal sanctuary, and the Duke has recently become actively involved in the plight of Britain's seal population, which in 1988 began to be severely attacked by a disease caused by marine pollution. In autumn 1988 he visited the Fame islands off the Northumberland coast, an area that formerly abounded with grey seals; he told Peter Harkey, who manages the islands for the National Trust, how concerned he was. Otters too are victims of this killer virus. Partly as a result of the publicity given by the Duke, money started pouring in to help those who run seal sanctuaries do what they can to help preserve these beautiful and threatened creatures.

Like many little girls, as a child the Duke's younger sister Alexandra lived, slept and talked nothing but horses. At one time she even refused any food that did not resemble oats, and in response to questions she would whinny and neigh! At the age of eight Alexandra won the prize for the best turned out pony at a local gymkhana, a task accomplished thanks to the use of an entire bottle of her mother's brilliantine. During the war, when she was growing up, she traded ponies with her cousins at Windsor – many animals went back and forwards in friendly exchange between Princess Alexandra and Princess Margaret.

Always keen on dogs, Alexandra took an early and active interest in the Guide Dogs for the Blind Association. When she married the Hon. Angus Ogilvy in 1963, this charity gave her one of her favourite wedding presents: four antique silver salt pots.

Left, *George, Duke of Kent, with his elder son Eddie, daughter Alexandra, and Chow at home at Coppins in Buckinghamshire. In 1942, George was killed in a wartime flying accident and his son became Duke of Kent.*

Below, *The Duke and Duchess of Kent at home in 1967 with their black labrador, Flint and Yorkshire terrier, Caspar.*

Left, *The Kent family at Anmer Hall on the Sandringham estate. Lord Nicholas Windsor on the pony, with George, Earl of St Andrews, and Lady Helen Windsor.*

Below, *Mother and daughter shared a love for dachshunds. Princess Marina with Princess Alexandra holding twelve-month old long-haired dachshund Mumphie.*

The Princess once said she would like to 'grow up like Mother, marry a farmer, give lots of cosy parties, hunt for five days a week . . .'. Like most people's childhood imaginings, reality has turned out to be more sober and down-to-earth. Nevertheless the Princess has been able to bring up her children, James and Marina, in the delightful surroundings of Thatched Lodge House in Richmond Park, where the deer emerge from the bracken to nibble the grass verges into a smooth carpet of green.

Angus Ogilvy is an excellent shot, and during a shooting lunch a guest once asked him how he felt about not taking the title of Earl when he married royalty. With a broad grin he replied that he never had any intention of doing so, but that sometimes when his children's nanny made a reverent curtsey in his wife's direction he could have reconsidered!

Princess Alexandra in fact has little time for unnecessary ceremony – she is a charming, natural person with a warm and caring personality. During an official trip to Japan she was being taken round a duck-netting site by the then Crown Prince. The pressmen wanted to photograph her with a bird in a net with its wing already broken. But the Princess chose to have an uninjured bird set free and only then asked for the pictures to be taken. That was typical of her thoughtfulness.

Prince and Princess Michael of Kent are unusual in being the only members of the royal family to keep cats. In fact when their family of Burmese cats were installed at Kensington Palace, they were said to have caused some consternation to the neighbours. Princess Margaret was reported to have complained at their howling and screaming at night, and Prince Charles gave orders that they were to be smartly ejected if caught scavenging in his kitchen.

But Princess Michael is devoted to the feline population, and when her first cat, Kitty, unaccountably went missing from the Palace in 1984, the incident hit the headlines. For some days the Princess cherished hopes that Kitty, who was a lover of car rides, had jumped into a strange car and been carried off by mistake. Unfortunately Kitty had been run over, and when her lifeless body was found the Princess was terribly distressed.

To help make up for the loss, Prince Michael gave her a pair of dark Burmese cats called Holly and Jessie, which were followed by a lighter Siamese called Magic. When asked on the popular radio programme *Desert Island Discs* what luxury she would like to take with her as a castaway, Princess Michael's immediate reply was: 'A cat.'

To marry the striking Austrian baroness, a divorcee and a Catholic, Prince Michael relinquished his right to the throne under the 1701 Act of Succession. The subject of much media attention, on account of both her family background and her extrovert personality, she has said that you can't be six feet tall and invisible.

Like his elder brother, the Duke of Kent, Prince Michael went to Sandhurst and was then commissioned into the 11th Hussars. He met MC, as Princess Michael – born Marie-Christine von Reibnitz – is known, at the Barnwell estate of his cousin, the Duke of Gloucester. They discovered that they both loved riding, and one of their first dates was on horseback in Richmond Park. Both believe a good gallop to be one of the best ways of coping with the stresses of life.

Prince Michael likes to be behind the reins of a carriage, and competes at Windsor driving events with Prince Philip. Princess Michael prefers the more energetic pursuits of hunting and eventing. She hunts with the Beaufort near their home in Gloucestershire, and takes part in the hunt's annual point-to-point. In 1983, she took up eventing, taking it seriously enough to say: 'I have trouble sleeping the night before I start. But when you're home after an exhilarating ride across country, it's a wonderful feeling.' She also took part in army horse trials at Tidworth, organized by the local hunt, competing in dressage, showjumping and cross-country racing. Princess Michael has taken a few tumbles out hunting, and in 1984 when her horse Sprite II tossed his head in the air, catching her a blow on the mouth, she responded by giving him a swift cuff on the nose. A spirited rider, she excelled in horsemanship when at school in Australia and was outstanding in all sports.

Nether Lypiatt Manor makes a relaxed and comfortable home for Prince and Princess Michael and their two children, Lord Frederick Windsor and Lady Gabriella Windsor, known as Ella. It is also home to numerous animals including two blue mountain goats, Ella's pony Rosie and two labradors. In the soft Gloucestershire countryside, Princess Michael's oriental cats with their glittering yellow eyes and graceful poses provide an exotic contrast. Each has a red collar with its name inscribed on a silver medal. Demanding and affectionate by turn, Jessie, Holly and Magic know how to make their presence felt – not unlike their owner.

Next-door neighbours to Prince and Princess Michael of Kent at Kensington Palace are the Duke and Duchess of Gloucester and their three children. A shy second son, Prince Richard of Gloucester was catapulted into being heir to this royal dukedom by the tragic death of his elder brother, Prince William, in a flying accident in 1972. Prince Richard had been at Cambridge only two days when he met the Danish-born Brigitte van Deurs, whom he was to marry. Together they make a valued team on whom the Queen can rely to represent her in a wide range of public duties.

The Gloucesters are not out to invite the limelight; and their

Above, *Princess Alexandra with puppy, Amber.*

Left, *This koala bear has already met the Queen, Prince Philip and the Queen Mother and on this occasion was brought to the ball room to be photographed with Princess Alexandra on her visit to Australia.*

Although the Queen longs for one of her horses to win the Derby, excitement was unconfined when she was joined by Prince and Princess Michael of Kent; the royal party cheered the Aga Khan's Khayasi as he won the great classic race.

children are probably among the least photographed of the younger royals. Lady Davina and Lady Rose once kept a rabbit in the garden of their Kensington Palace apartment; but he was said to be terrorized by Princess Michael's cats, and had to be removed to the Gloucesters' country home in Northamptonshire.

Among the good causes supported by the Gloucesters is St John of Jerusalem, of which the Duke is Grand Prior. At one of their dinners, held in the Mansion House in London, he confided in me about a new family acquisition: 'We've got a new puppy, a cavalier called Barley.' Asked if the spaniel puppy would get on well with their other dogs, he replied: 'We haven't had any for a long time now. This is very special to us, after not having had a dog for several years. It's got very long, caramel-coloured ears. . . .' As he carried himself off into a private reverie at the very thought of this delightful picture of puppyhood, it was obvious that the Duke, eyes twinkling behind his spectacles, had been well smitten by Barley. It must run in the family: his father was so attached to his dogs that when he went into the army he took two of them with him.

Cavaliers have a courageous and faithful nature, and problems only arise when they are treated as soft: without proper exercise they tend to become pampered and overweight. But with Andrew Patrick, Earl of Ulster, now a teenager, and the active Davina and Rose, exercise should not be a problem on the 2500-acre Barnwell Manor estate near Peterborough, where the family spend as much of their time as possible. From the windows of the historic house, which dates from

Right, *Henry, Duke of Gloucester at the Adelaide Koala Bear Farm, South Australia in 1934*

Below, *When her horse, Sprite II tossed his head, catching Princess Michael a blow on the mouth, the Princess responded with a swift cuff on the nose.*

The Duke and Duchess of Gloucester at Barnwell Manor with labrador Tarqua and three of their Australian terriers.

1264, they can look out over a landscape of green pastures and grazing cattle.

All the Gloucester children enjoy riding; and the Duke takes his son to shoot game. The present Duke's father bought the estate in 1938, and set about modernizing the farm. It consists mainly of arable land, and until recently was not particularly rich in game. Shooting was generally of the family-friends-and-neighbours kind when Prince Richard was a boy, and no gamekeepers were employed. But Richard has improved the shoot and now takes an active interest in gamekeeping.

A practising architect, the Duke still manages to find time for other activities. He is a Ranger of Epping Forest and President of the East of England Agricultural Society; as a Fellow of the Royal Society of Architects he has combined his knowledge of architecture with his interest in the conservation of nature. In line with the feelings expressed by an increasing number of members of the royal family, he has spent time teaching his children to respect the natural habitats of forest creatures, to preserve woodlands, and to safeguard endangered species such as the golden plover and the otter. There cannot be a better philosophy to instill into the next generation at a time when the planet could be facing destruction caused by man's own unthinking folly.

FURTHER READING

AIRLIE, Mabell, Countess of, *Thatched with Gold*, Hutchinson, 1962
ARONSON, Theo, *The King in Love*, John Murray
ASQUITH, Lady Cynthia, *Diaries*, 1937
BATTISCOMBE, Georgina, *Queen Alexandra*, Constable
BLOCH, Michael, *Letters of Wallis and Edward*
BOOTHROYD, Basil, *Philip*, Longman
BROUGH, James, *Margaret, the Tragic Princess*, G. P. Putnam
CAMPBELL, Judith, *The Queen Rides*, Lutterworth
CAMPBELL, Judith, *Royal Horses*, New English Library
CARTLAND, Barbara, *Book of Royal Days*, 1988
CATHCART, Helen, *Sandringham*, W. H. Allen, 1964
CATHCART, Helen, *The Queen and the Turf*, Stanley Paul
CATHCART, Helen, *Anne, The Princess Royal*, W. H. Allen
CHANCE, Michael, *Our Princesses and Their Dogs*, John Murray
CLAYTON, Michael, *Prince Charles, Horseman*, Stanley Paul, 1987
COOLICAN, Don, *The Queen Mother*, Scott, 1986
COWLES, Virginia, *Edward VII and His Circle*, Hamish Hamilton, 1956
CRAWFORD, Marion, *The Little Princesses*, Cassell, 1950
CURLING, *British Racecourses*, Witherby
DALY, MacDonald, *Royal Dogs*, W. H. Allen, 1952
DE BALLAIGUE, Geoffrey, Oliver Millar and John Harris, *Buckingham Palace*, Collins
DONALDSON, Frances, *Edward VIII*, Weidenfeld & Nicolson
DUFF, David, *Elizabeth of Glamis*, Muller, 1973
ELBORG, Geoffrey, *Princess Alexandra*, Sheldon Press, 1982
FISHER, Heather and Graham, *Prince Andrew*, W. H. Allen, 1981
FISHER, Heather and Graham, *Consort*, W. H. Allen, 1980
FISHER, Heather and Graham, *The Queen's Travels*, Robert Hale, 1985
FISHER, Heather and Graham, *Monarch*, Robert Hale, 1987
FOYSTER, Bernard, *Princess Anne*, Arlington Books, 1972
GOW, Michael, *Trooping the Colour*, Souvenir Press
HIGHAM, Charles, *Wallis*, Sidgwick & Jackson, 1988
HOEY, Brian, *Monarchy*, BBC Publications
HOLDEN, Anthony, *Charles*, Weidenfeld & Nicolson, 1979
HRH PRINCESS MARIE LOUISE, *My Memories of Six Reigns*, Evans, 1956
JUDD, Denis, *King George VI*, Michael Joseph, 1982
KING, Stella, *Princes Marina*, Cassell
LACEY, Robert, *Majesty*, Hutchinson, 1981
LANE, Peter, *Prince Philip*, Robert Hale, 1981
LANE, Peter, *Princess Michael of Kent*, Robert Hale, 1986
LONGFORD, Elizabeth, *Victoria RI*, Weidenfeld & Nicolson
LONGRIGG, Roger, *The History of Fox Hunting*, Macmillan, 1975
MACKENZIE, Compton, *The Windsor Tapestry*, The Book Club, 1932
MAGNUS, Sir Philip, *King Edward VII*, Weidenfeld & Nicolson, 1964
MARSHALL, J. H., *Horseman*, Bodley Head, 1970
MASSIE, Robert, *The Last Courts of Europe*, Dent, 1981
MIDDLEMAS, Keith, *Edward VII*, Weidenfeld & Nicolson
MONTAGUE-SMITH, Kidde, *Debrett's Book of Royal Children*, Debrett's Books
MORTON, Andrew, *Duchess*, Michael O'Mara
NICHOLSON, Harold, *King George the Fifth, His Life and Reign*, Doubleday

PONSONBY, Sir Frederick, *Recollections of Three Reigns*, Quartet
POPE-HENNESSEY, James, *Queen Mary*, George Allen & Unwin, 1959
PYE, Michael, *The King Across the Water*, Holt, Rinehart & Winston, 1981
REID, Michaela, *Ask Sir James*, Hodder & Stoughton, 1987
RIPPON, Angela, *Mark Phillips*, David & Charles
ROSE, Kenneth, *King George V*, Weidenfeld & Nicolson, 1983
ST AUBYN, Giles, *Edward VII, Prince and King*, Collins
SHAKERLEY, Sir Geoffrey, Felicity Wigan and Victoria Mather, *The English Dog at Home*, Chatto & Windus, 1986
SHAKESPEARE, Nicholas, *The Men Who Would be King*, Sidgwick & Jackson
SITWELL, Edith, *The Queens and the Hive*, Macmillan, 1962
STRACHEY, Lytton, *The Illustrated Queen Victoria*, Bloomsbury
STRONG, Roy, *Cecil Beaton: The Royal Portraits*, Thames & Hudson, 1988
WARWICK, Christopher, *King George VI & Queen Elizabeth*, Sidgwick & Jackson, 1985
WARWICK, Christopher, *Abdication*, Sidgwick & Jackson, 1986
WHITLOCK, Ralph, *Royal Farmers*, Michael Joseph
WINDSOR, HRH The Duke of, *A King's Story*, Cassell, 1951
WINDSOR, The Duchess of, *The Heart has its Reasons*, Michael Joseph, 1956

INDEX

Compiled by M. J. Heary

PICTURE CREDITS

Black and White